SCM for
Network Development
Environments

SCM for
Network Development
Environments

Joseph H. Rawlings III

McGraw-Hill, Inc.

New York   San Francisco   Washington, D.C.   Auckland   Bogotá
Caracas   Lisbon   London   Madrid   Mexico City   Milan
Montreal   New Delhi   San Juan   Singapore
Sydney   Tokyo   Toronto

Library of Congress number: 93-39215

2 3 4 5 6 7 8 9 0   DOC/DOC   9 9 8 7 6 5 4

ISBN 0-07-051101-2

The sponsoring editor for this book was Jeanne Glasser, the editing supervisor was Fred Dahl, and the production supervisor was Donald F. Schmidt. This book was set in Century Schoolbook by Inkwell Publishing Services.

Printed and bound by R. R. Donnelley & Sons Company.

I dedicate this book to my loving wife.
The best Genies don't come in a bottle.

Contents

x   Contents

Preface

It is the intention of this book to provide a fundamental understanding of configuration management concepts and techniques. The intent is not only to describe the concepts and techniques, but to show how they are implemented using the PVCS product series from INTERSOLV Inc.

Various configuration management techniques and strategies are presented along with pragmatic applications thereof in the networked software development environment. Methods for preventing problems are described as well as procedures for fixing them. Time-saving methods are described for controlling and maintaining the software development environment.

The reader will learn how to define and implement customized secure environments using the PVCS Series' enhanced access control security system. The development of a project hierarchy is described, as is revision, version, release, and promotion management.

The PVCS Series Tool set was selected because of its vast popularity and its excellent implementation of configuration management tools.

Trademark Credits

INTERSOLV and PVCS are trademarks of INTERSOLV, Inc.

MS-DOS, Windows, and Microsoft are registered trademarks of Microsoft Corporation.

Netware is a registered trademark of Novell Inc.

PC-DOS, Presentation Manager, OS/2, IBM, and AD/Cycle are trademarks of IBM Corporation.

UNIX is a registered trademark of AT&T Corporation.

Thompson Toolkit is a trademark of Thompson Automation, Inc.

All other products are trademarks and/or registered trademarks of their respective companies.

Acknowledgments

I would like to express my deepest appreciation to my good friend Jim Stewart for all his help and advice. I would also like to thank Jonathan Toland, Steve Lehto, and John Tracey of INTERSOLV, Inc. and Pat Thompson of Thompson Automation Inc. for all their kind assistance. Most of all, I would like to thank my wife for tolerating my prolonged journeys into my dungeon.

Joseph H. Rawlings III

SCM for
Network Development
Environments

Common Problems in Software Development

Communications Breakdown

It is a wonderful experience to be a member of a team that has set out to conquer a problem and provide a clean and easy to use solution, or to produce a software application having a clean and easy-to-use interface with elegant data handling. A common bond forms between each and every one of the team members. That common bond is the desire to produce a quality product, on time, and within budget. A product that the marketplace will love and purchase. A product that will provide profitability to the company that sponsored the team and rewards to the team members.

However glorious the picture may seem, there are also some drawbacks to working in a team environment. The primary drawback, and the cause of most team and product problems, is interteam communications. When only one person is working on a project, that one person has a rather singular communication path with no need for interpretative cognition. The person has only him or herself to communicate with and, hopefully, understands his or her own though processes. When two people are working on the same project, there are now two communicators and two listeners with four potential communication paths. Not only is there a dramatic increase in the number of communication paths, there is also the problem of interpretive cognition, which now comes into play.

Interpretive cognition is the process of reconstructing an abstract concept by interpreting ambiguous symbols. When a human attempts to communicate an idea, he or she must first describe the idea using words as symbols that when combined in the appropriate manner, represent the idea. The listener hears the words and uses the words as symbols to construct a model of the communicated idea. When the listener fails to interpret the symbols correctly, one of two things will occur: either the listener will assume that he or she has interpreted the symbols correctly and proceed on a false premise, or he or she will invoke a feedback loop. Occasionally the speaker will feel that the listener does not understand, even though the listener thinks he or she does, and will invoke the feedback loop on his or her own. In this feedback loop the communication process reverses. The listener assumes the role of speaker and transmits his or her own set of symbols to the original speaker who now becomes the listener. This loop continues until the listener is sure that he or she has the idea or the speaker is sure that the listener has correctly interpreted the idea. This process is illustrated in Fig. 1.1. Feedback from the listener to the speaker is essential for correct interpretive cognition, and ultimately, comprehension. Between any two people there are really four communications paths, two originating paths and two feedback paths. Without great care and

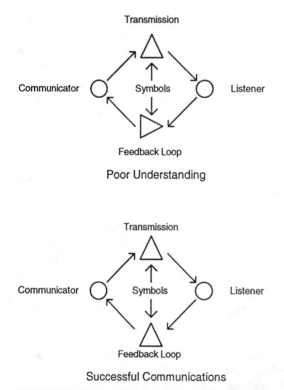

Figure 1.1   A communications model.

attention, any one of the four communications paths may break down at any time resulting in confusion and miscommunication.

As more and more people are added to a conversation, the total number of communications paths increases dramatically as does the potential for comprehension errors. Figure 1.2 illustrates the logarithmic growth of communications paths as more communicators are added.

When you were a child in grade school, you probably participated in a communications experiment to show just how unreliable the verbal communication process is. The experiment required that all participants form a single-file line. The experiment began with the first person in line secretly writing down a phrase on a piece of paper and then turning and whispering that phrase into the second person's ear. The second person then immediately whispered the phrase into the third person's ear. This process continued until all participants had listened to and then passed on the phrase as they understood it. The last person in the line, (and the last to hear the phrase), then spoke it aloud. The person who made up the original phrase then told the class what was originally said. No matter how hard the participants tried, the last person never said exactly what the first person had written. What the experiment demonstrated is that left to themselves and unattended, communications tend toward decay and eventual self-destruction.

Transmittal of simple ideas is complicated enough, but how do you control communications in the complex software development process? How can you keep everyone informed of every task that both affects them and is in progress? How can you track each interrelated activity and object? How can you prevent people from duplicating effort or

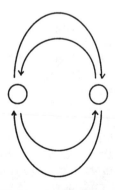

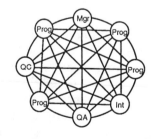

4 Communication Paths   116 Communications Paths

Figure 1.2   (Left) Two-person conversation; (Right) Eight-person conversation.

damaging work already accomplished by others? How do you prevent communications breakdowns from creating general confusion?

There are three ways to solve the communications breakdown problem. The first is to have every person tell every other person what it is that they are going to do and how long it will take them. Each person must ensure that his or her work will not interfere with any other persons work. Using this approach, with diligence, no communications paths break down, and unfortunately, no work gets done. Everyone spends all of their time talking and listening to every other team member. Not only is this an impossible solution to implement, it has no practical value whatsoever.

The second method of solving the communications problem is to provide basic communications and then hope that the right people will tell the next level of right people just what is happening and when. Trusting to blind luck is definitely neither a scientific nor a reasonable solution to the problem, so policies and procedures are implemented as controls to minimize the potential for error. Yet even with controls in place, many things can go wrong. The control solution is the approach to the communications problem that most organizations must take because it is just too expensive and time-consuming to approach a solution to the problem in any other way.

The third method of solving the communications problem is to employ software development tools and techniques that mandate, either implicitly or explicitly, the communications required to effectively control the development process. These tools provide automatic communication to the members of the team without the need for meetings and hallway conversations to discuss, in detail, planned activities and the time schedules for each. These software tools provide a path to solving the communications problem through configuration management.

Let us examine an example of how software development tools can be used to provide automated team communication. The software tool used in this example is a revision control and tracking program. When programmer "A" needs to edit a code module, he or she must first extract a working copy of the module. Assume that programmer "B" is already editing the same module. When programmer A attempts to extract a copy of the module for editing purposes, the revision control tool reports to the programmer that the module is already being edited by someone else, in this case programmer B. Programmer A has received a communication from programmer B even though programmer B is completely unaware that the communication occurred. It was the revision control tool that initiated and provided the communication. A communications path between the programmers was automatically generated.

Three Classic Problems

Despite all the controls, policies, procedures, and methods that have been implemented over the years in the software development arena, there are three classic problems that have been encountered in one form or another by nearly every programming team. These problems are common to mainframe computer developers, minicomputer developers, networked computer developers, and personal computer developers. They are not operating-system dependent, although some operating systems do attempt to minimize them or their effect. These classic problems can arise whenever two or more people share any common resources. These problems are:

1. The shared data problem
2. The multiple maintenance problem
3. The simultaneous update problem

The shared data problem

The shared data problem arises when a single file or program module can be accessed by more than one person or can be referenced by more than one software system for any one of a multitude of reasons. For example, a program module that implements a function that is called by several other program modules is a likely candidate to experience the shared data problem.

Sometimes a program module is modified to enhance the operation of another program module. The modification for one program module may cause errors in, or total failure of, another program module that calls or invokes the modified module.

In Fig. 1.3, there are two programs that access the function provided in program module "C". If a programmer from the team assigned to program 1 edits module C to solve a problem experienced by program 1, the impact upon program 2 may be severe if not fatal. For example, if the programmer from the team assigned to program 1 added a parameter to the call to module C, then program 2 has the potential to crash when it reaches a point where it makes a call to the function contained in module C. A program crash may occur if a parameter is removed from the calling sequence. Whether or not adding or subtracting a parameter will cause a program crash is a function of the compiler's ordering of the parameters on the stack, which is out of the programmer's control.

The most difficult aspect of this problem is that none of the programmers associated with program 2 are likely to realize just what the new problem is with their program. "It worked yesterday, I just don't

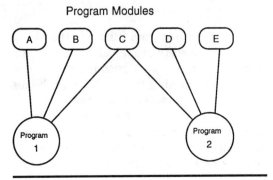

Figure 1.3 Shared data problem.

understand why it should fail today" is a common lament. Many hours of debugging later it is discovered that module *C* has a new parameter. After sweeping up all the torn-out hair and discarding it in the appropriate receptacle, the team leader can calm down enough to confront the program 1 team leader and discuss the communications breakdown that led to several nervous breakdowns and an extremely upset product manager.

Solving the shared data problem

The original solution to the Shared Data Problem was the creation of separate and individual workspaces. Each program had its own copy of each module and could modify them without fear of negative impact upon any other program. The workspace solution is used today by many software development teams and provides a minimal resolution to the shared data problem. Unfortunately, it also creates another problem.

The multiple maintenance problem

The multiple maintenance problem is encountered when there are multiple copies of the same module. The first problem with multiple module copies is tracking them. What programs use which copy of each and every module? Where is this particular copy used? Which copy of the module is used with that program?

The second problem with multiple copies is tracking the differences between the various copies of each and every module. How and why is one copy different from another? This leads to the question, "Who is responsible for this mess anyway?"

The third and biggest problem with using multiple copies of a module lies in maintaining all of the various copies. What happens if a bug is found in one of the copies? Do they all have the bug? How can you know? If they do, how can you verify the repair of the bug in all copies? Can you even find all of the copies? How do you know you've found all the copies when you think you have? Are you really sure?

In Fig. 1.4, there are six working copies of a single module used in two programs. Three are associated with three separate subsystems of program 1. The other three copies are associated with three separate subsystems of program 2. Each of the three copies associated with program 1 may be different from one another, as each is used in a different subsystem by different programmers on the same team. The same is true for the three copies associated with program 2. If a programmer finds a bug in his or her own copy of the module, then there is the distinct chance that each and every other copy of the same module has the exact same bug.

Acting in good faith and in the interest of the project, the programmer who found the bug would probably tell everyone he or she knew who used the module about the bug. Did the programmer in fact do so? Can you guarantee that all programmers know of all other programmers who use the same modules? What happens if program 2 is developed by a team at a completely different site? Do all programmers know of all applications that use any given module? There are too many questions and not nearly enough good answers.

Solving the multiple maintenance problem

The original solution to the multiple maintenance problem was the creation of "baselines." Any module that required different implementations was broken up into the required implementations and each given a different name. All modules were then stored in a central location, the *baseline*.

All programs drew modules as required from the baseline. This guaranteed that any module would be consistent from one program to the next. If a bug was discovered in a module, the baseline copy was

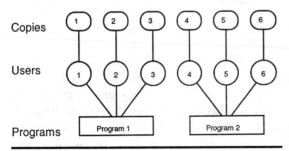

Figure 1.4   Multiple maintenance program.

repaired and the repair was thus automatically available and distributed to all the users of that module. Baselines were the precursor to today's libraries and repositories.

Unfortunately, the baseline solution did nothing to address the need for small custom changes to modules for particular application requirements. Multiple application ports to different equipment platforms were not practical. Custom releases for specific customers were ill advised. Additionally, the mechanics of updating the baseline copy led to the discovery of the third classic problem, the simultaneous update problem.

The simultaneous update problem

The simultaneous update problem may surface whenever two authors attempt to modify the same module at the same time. On the surface, it appears that this problem should be a minor one. How often do two editors access the same file at the same time? In practice, the simultaneous edit of a single file occurs much more often than one would believe. Have you ever gone to edit a file or examine a database and it just didn't look right? You look a little closer. "Wait a minute, didn't I edit this last week?" "I'm sure I did!" Where did the changes go? You figure they went to the big bit bucket in the sky, then you shrug your shoulders and reenter the changes. Where did they go? If you look very hard and communicate with the other developers, you will most likely find that the changes were lost due to the simultaneous update problem.

The simultaneous update problem is particularly nasty and has been the cause of many a bad release. It has produced problems so severe that the repercussions have caused total company failure in more than one case. The simultaneous edit can occur over a long period of time. An author that takes several weeks to make an edit and then proceeds to upload it may destroy the work of many editors.

Figure 1.5 illustrates the events and conditions that may lead to the simultaneous update problem. Fortunately, there are three conditions that must be met for the problem to arise. Unfortunately, these three conditions are realized far too often during the software life cycle for any given module.

The first requirement is that two or more authors edit the same file at the same time. In the case of two simultaneous authors, both acquire a copy of the file from the baseline. Both make their modifications to the file. The first one done copies his or her completed work back into the baseline. Then the second one done copies his or her completed work back into the baseline. Unfortunately, the copy edited by the second author does not contain the work of the first author. When the second author copies his or her revision up to the baseline, the first author's work is overwritten and lost.

The problem is illustrated in Fig. 1.5 where the first author modifies module revision "A" to create module revision "A1". The second author modifies module revision A to create module revision "A2". When the first author completes his or her edit, (in our case, author #1), the new revision of module A, revision A1 is copied back into the baseline where it is now considered safe and generally accessible. The new copy of the module overwrites the old copy of the module, loosely speaking, revision A becomes revision A1. When the second author completes his or her edit and checks his or her new copy (revision A2) into the baseline, revision A1 is completely written over by the new copy, revision A2. All the changes made by the first author are lost forever. The worst part of the problem is that the first author does not even realize that his or her work has been lost.

Solving the simultaneous update problem

The solution to the simultaneous update problem is simple. File locking allows access by just one user at a time. The lock stores the name of the author so that only the author who owns the lock can check in a new copy. Only one edit copy of a module is permitted. When an author is done with his or her edit and checks his or her copy back into the baseline, the lock is removed and the next author may then proceed to edit by checking out and locking the baseline copy of the module. No one author can overwrite another author's changes. In effect, file locking is an automatic communications mechanism that says to all other authors, "the module is being edited, please wait your turn."

Drawbacks to Existing Solutions

There are a number of drawbacks to the above described solutions to the three classic problems. Workspaces may cure the shared data

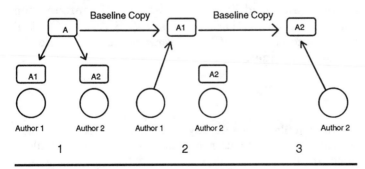

Figure 1.5 The simultaneous update problem.

problem, but they introduce the multiple maintenance problem. Base-lines cure the multiple maintenance problem, but do not readily permit customization of modules for a given application or customer. Baseli-nes also introduce the simultaneous update problem. Locks cure the simultaneous update problem, but do not permit simultaneous work. Access to the file must be serialized and locks do not provide a mechanism by which custom modifications can be accomplished.

How can file access be paralleled in order to solve problems on time? How can a custom release for the biggest and best customer be made? How can you manage a multiple hardware platform project? How do you assign serialized work in a parallel manner so that everyone is kept busy all the time?

Configuration Management

The task of configuration management is to address the classic problems, overcome communication obstacles and provide useful information to its users. Before addressing the classic problems, some fundamental problems require solution. The first fundamental problem that needs to be overcome is that of communication break-down. To effectively communicate, each member of any conversation needs to know what the word symbols used by all other members of the conversation really mean. In other words, a common vocabulary is essential to good communications. Unfortunately, even today, many organizations give their own name to the exact same concept that another organization may call by yet another name. In order to prevent confusion and to establish good communications, some concept definitions will be provided so that we are all speaking the same language. Do not be concerned if the nomenclature does not exactly match that found in your work environment as it is highly unlikely that any one organization or culture has all the same terms for the same things as any other organization or culture. The following definitions are used in several commercial configuration management products such as INTERSOLV's "PVCS Version Control System" otherwise known as the *PVCS*® *Version Manager*, and the "PVCS Configuration Builder."

Definitions

MODULE: A program file. A module may be a requirements document, a source code file, a section of a user manual contained in its own file, a configuration file, a file of test data, a test script, a makefile, a build script or any other type of file.

REVISION: An instance of a module. If you edit a module and change it in any way, the result is a new instance or revision of the module. Revisions track the sequential evolution of a module.

SYSTEM: What it is that you are constructing. The system may be what ships when you sell a product. It may be a subsystem. It may be a subsystem of a subsystem. It may be a user manual, one or more executable programs, one or more data files, test files, product specifications, or product requirements. A system is made up of components. The components are modules.

VERSION: An instance of a system or the system at a given point in time. For example, it may be the "alpha release" version, the test version, the development version, the custom release for company "XYZ" version. A version could represent a milestone or some other desired reference point in the system's life cycle.

RELEASE: A release occurs when a version of the product is put up for sale or put into official use. The first release of the product may be the *beta release* followed by the first public offering of the product, *Release 1.0*.

ARCHIVE FILE: The baseline or archive copy of a module. An archive file maintains all revisions of the module and associates versions with revisions. Additionally the archive file maintains a wealth of information about the file such as the names of all the authors, the dates of file modification, the author's comments about the changes, a file description, and much more. This set of information is sometimes called a change history. An archive file is maintained by a revision or version control system and is never edited by an author. A collection of archive files is used to represent an entire system.

WORKFILE: A workfile is a working copy of a revision of a module that has been "checked out" of an archive file for editing purposes. It is owned by the person who checked it out and may be edited by that person only. Any changes made during an edit will be accepted into the archive file when the author checks in the new revision into the archive file. This can only happen if the author checked out the working copy with a lock.

JOURNAL: An audit trail file that maintains a centralized listing of all activity related to any archive file under its control or jurisdiction. A given project may have one or more journal files as required. The journal is not a mandatory file but it is highly recommended that one be used.

TRUNK: The trunk of an archive file is the main development path of the module. Each succeeding revision is added to the trunk by default unless otherwise specified.

BRANCH: An archive file uses a branch to track alternate or parallel development paths. For example, if a custom modification is required for a given customer, that modification to the main development path is maintained on a branch. In another example, the revisions created during the port of an application to a different platform would be maintained on a branch.

TIP: The latest revision to be checked into the trunk or a branch of the archive file. The tip of the trunk is accessed by default when archive file operations occur as the tip is the most active or likely to change or grow. The tip may sometimes be called a leaf.

OWNER: The owner of an archive file is the entity that possesses the archive file. The owner may be a person or it may be a project name. For simplicity in report generation, using a project name rather than a person's name may be preferred.

AUTHOR: The person who checks in a revision is the author of that revision. Typically, the author is the person who created the file or who made changes to the file. Each revision has its own author.

New solutions to old problems

Using the above definitions, it becomes easy to see how to solve the three classic problems. We solve the shared data problem and enhance the original solution by implementing archive files with branches as illustrated in Fig. 1.6. If a module requires a special modification for a special purpose, a branch is created to track the special changes. The trunk and each branch of an archive file corresponds to the separate workspaces in the original solution. The workspace for all programs without special requirements is the trunk of the archive file. The workspace for an alternative, ported, or special program is a single branch of the archive file.

The multiple maintenance problem is also solved using archive files. The collection of archive files that represents the system corresponds to a multidimensional baseline as illustrated in Fig. 1.7. When any

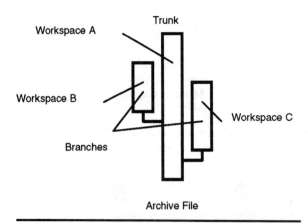

Figure 1.6 Shared data solution.

Programs

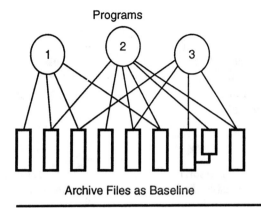

Archive Files as Baseline

Figure 1.7   Multiple maintenance solution.

module (or branch thereof) is updated, all authors and programs that access that module (or branch thereof) are updated automatically the next time that they access the archive file baseline.

The simultaneous update problem is solved by locks as before. Because the archive file maintains multiple revisions and multiple branches of a code module, multiple instances of the same module may exist as shown in Fig. 1.8. Simultaneous edits of different revisions of the same file can occur without adverse impact upon each other. Unless special parameters are invoked, no one revision may be edited by more than one author and no one author may edit multiple revisions of a single module, however, multiple revisions can be edited by multiple authors on a one-to-one basis.

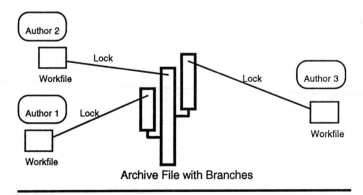

Figure 1.8   Enhanced simultaneous update solution.

Summary

Complete and accurate communication between the members of a team is nearly impossible. As a result, errors can occur and problems arise. The problems can be overcome and errors can be minimized by employing configuration management techniques that use existing and readily available software tools.

Questions

Sometimes, managers (with good reason) prefer to play their cards close to their chests. They are secretive. Information from higher-level management flows down the hierarchical chain until the secretive manager becomes an informational dam. The secretive manager prevents the flow of information from reaching the trenches from which spring the company product.

1. How does this information block affect the team communication process? How could it have a positive effect on the team? What negative effects could it have on the project? How can the team overcome obstacles presented by this management style? How can configuration management techniques help the team in this context?

2. Write down your answers and save them. The answers to these questions and more will be found in later chapters. Compare your thoughts now to those you have when you have completed this book. Determine how and why your opinions changed.

2

What Is Configuration Management?

A Dynamic Global Perspective

There are many perspectives of a project. The perspective taken by a team member depends upon the responsibilities and goals of that member. The view of the project taken by a project manager will differ from the view taken by a developer. The view taken by a systems integrator will differ from that taken by a software quality assurance person.

There are many aspects to the software development process. To gain control of a software project and to accomplish a viable working development environment, some kind of definition must be established for each and every aspect of the development process. A level of information granularity must be decided upon and then enforced.

Project definition

In the software life cycle, the first phase of project development is the design phase. Project specifications and requirements documents are produced. Decisions are made concerning the functionality of the product, its target market, its user interface, and other critical issues. Functional specifications are created. Hopefully, at the same time that these critical components are defined, testing procedures and methods are defined and plans for the documentation are started. The project itself is defined during the design phase.

In an ideal world, these requirements and specifications would be static and unchanging, but reality is far from ideal and specifications and requirements are not set in stone. As more is learned about implementing the project, specifications and functional requirements change to enhance the product. Customer desires are considered and cause further alteration of specifications. Almost every software project experiences modification of its basic definitions at least once.

The problem with specification alteration is that everyone involved needs to know what the changes are when they occur. All too often, a developer will complete a source code module based upon an out-of-date specification. Why? Is it because nobody told the developer about the change? Was the change made after the developer began to implement the code and the developer never checked to see if the specification changed? When confronted with a specification change after completing the code, the developer may well claim that the code complies to the copy of the specification that they had in hand. Has the multiple maintenance problem surfaced? Has lack of communication frustrated the developer? How much time, effort, and money was wasted in developing an out-of-date system?

Source code

The ultimate goal of the project is to produce a software system composed of one or more software subsystems, each of which is constructed from source code modules. Each of these modules will change several times during the development process. Bugs get fixed. Algorithms are redesigned. Specifications change. Most of these modules will have some kind of interface to other source code modules. How can you accurately track the relationships? Do you draw diagrams indicating the relationships of one module to another? How do you maintain such a drawing? How do you include revisions of the modules in the diagram?

Project Perspective

The perspective of the project taken by a developer is completely different from that taken by a system integrator, manager, marketer, and even another fellow developer.

A large software project may consist of thousands of modules interconnected in a very complicated manner. A large software project may be created by combining software systems, each is different from the other. A developer whose concern is the user interface will have a different view of the project than a developer whose concern is the internals of an operating kernel. The perspective of each and every individual connected with the project will differ from every other team member if only from sheer necessity. Personal interests, desires, experience, and characteristics create further diversity in the perspectives taken by the various individuals who belong on the development team.

Regardless of differences in perspective, providing a view of the project for each individual that adheres to the individual's needs and desires is a fundamental necessity. It is configuration management's job to meet the views of all team members. Each individual feels that their view of the project is the most important and relevant view. If the software development tools that are in use by a software development organization are incapable of providing a dynamic view of the project, then at least one individual or set of individuals will feel that his or her very important perspective of the project is being ignored. The individual's needs are not being met.

One of the basic paradigms of configuration management is that it provide a dynamic perspective of the project. To accomplish this task, the entire project must be considered in the global sense. From requirements and specifications to components, documentation and tests to the final product, each element of the project is as important as any other element.

To further exacerbate the problem, each of the elements of the project is subject to change. Source code is not the only alterable factor in a software project. In fact, nearly every element will change in one way or another during the project life cycle. As changes occur, the project changes. The view of the project must change as well. A static view of the project will surely cause failure to some degree.

Every project is different

Some projects are completely self-contained. The self-contained project relates in no way to any other project. Each element of the project is unique to the project. This does not preclude complexity. The self-contained project may be large and very complicated.

Some projects make use of materials, ideas, code, or specifications that are or were used in another project. Tracking these "borrowed" elements and any required modifications to them adds complexity to the task of controlling the project.

Some projects consist of more than one subproject, each of which may borrow from no, some, or all other subprojects. Multiple projects are the hardest to manage and maintain, even with configuration management techniques. It is most likely that such projects are nearly impossible to manage effectively without configuration management techniques.

Group dynamics are different

Another factor to consider is the composition of the team. Not all the members of a team need the same information or privileges. Certain tasks are not appropriate for some team members. A person whose job it is to test a program probably should not be able to alter the user documentation for the program. A developer with six months experience does not necessarily have the knowledge to be able to define accurately what changes to a specification should occur.

What about security? Should all members of the team have equal access to project information? What about marketing? Management? Consultants? Not only do specifications and code change over the software life cycle, personnel change as well. People acquire new skill sets and responsibilities. People leave the project. New people are brought on board. These questions will be resolved later in this book in the discussion of the access control database.

No two programming teams share the exact same characteristics. Teams are composed of individuals with differing personalities, talents, knowledge, and desires. If no two people are exactly the same, then no two teams can possibly be identical.

Teams are composed of individuals who differ in the professional sense as well. Some members have vast experience and knowledge. Other members may be fresh out of school and have very little experience. Assigning tasks and responsibilities to an inexperienced team member that are better suited for an experienced team member may not be appropriate. Providing the new team member with the same access rights as an experienced team member may even be a serious mistake.

Environments are different

Each work place is different. Some enjoy vast freedom with minimal security requirements. Some have very specific security needs. Some are loosely knit with personnel playing many roles. Some are tightly defined with specific tasks and responsibilities for each team member.

The small microcomputer-based company that has grown into the need for a networked development environment will have a completely different set of needs than the mainframe-based company that has downsized or off-loaded the mainframe development to a local area network (LAN). Yet the fundamental needs for project tracking and control are identical for both situations.

The culture of a company is also a factor. Some companies may have started off using a collection of microcomputers or workstations with no interconnection other than floppy disk. Others may have started off using mainframes. The cultural background of a company has a great deal to do with the perspectives of a project taken by team members.

A perspective of the entire project, including personnel, that changes with the project and adapts to the needs of the user is necessary. Rigorous configuration management policies and procedures will provide this dynamic global perspective.

The Perspective Granularity

Different groups of personnel have different needs when the global perspective of the project is considered. A developer may need to know about the various revisions of a source code module. The project manager may need to know about various versions or releases of the project. Higher level management or marketing may only want to know about released products. The granularity of information differs for each user. The developer requires a more intimate view, that is, a fine granularity, the project manager does not.

There are tradeoffs that must be decided upon when configuration management techniques are first employed. Will a single database meet our needs? What level of granularity is required in a database to produce information of relevance? The nature of the project, the environment, company policy and the software life cycle all influence the decisions that must be made. However, in the final analysis, to provide flexibility and a growth path, the same tool set should be used to satisfy simple needs or complex requirements.

The point is that the configuration management database structure should be adaptable and variable. An organization should be able to define and implement both the nature and the granularity of their tracking system to serve the specific project requirements.

Variable perspective

One of the advantages of formal configuration management is that it allows users to define the granularity of their own perspective. A developer should be able to find out about the differences in the revisions of a single source code module. A change history for a module should be readily accessible. Using the tools that make up the configuration management environment, the developer can easily do so. An integration engineer may need to know the differences between one release and another. The same tool set that the developer used to find revision differences for a single module should be able to provide information about release differences in all modules to the integration engineer.

Obtaining perspective

Configuration management is a combination of tools and techniques for controlling the software development process and is implemented using software tools of differing natures. The tools used are the same for all personnel, regardless of position or responsibility.

By using various options of the tool set, individuals acquire a perspective of the project suited to their particular needs. For example, if a developer needs to find the exact differences between two revisions of a source code module, then a tool that displays such differences would be employed. The developer would invoke the tool using the two revisions as parameters. The same tool could be used to determine the differences between the specifications for two release levels by passing the two release levels as parameters at the tool's invocation.

Using a single tool set, every need of each team member can be met as long as the tools used are adaptable. A good configuration management tool set should not require that the working environment be altered to conform to requirements specified by the tools. The tool set should be adaptable to the environment. The tools should provide a vast functionality, enabling the user to match his or her needs, whether the user is a developer, documentation editor, project manager, or test engineer.

Enforced granularity

On the other side of the coin is the minimal granularity necessary to provide the required information. Minimal granularity means the smallest amount of change information required to be stored to accomplish a given task. To accomplish minimal granularity, every modification of each module, regardless of the content or type of module, must be tracked. If only release levels are tracked, it becomes very difficult to track working versions. If working versions are the lowest level of granularity, then engineers and developers may not be able to recover gracefully from failed experiments or inadvertent coding errors.

Formal configuration management does not mandate the granularity that is to be implemented. The tools that are used to implement configuration management may be used in whatever fashion is desired. However, for configuration management to be an effective tool for each member of the team, the organization should make use of the tool to the finest level of granularity possible. Each and every change made to any module, regardless of the significance of the change, should be recorded and commented. Only then will you attain sufficient granularity to meet the needs of the various team functions.

Voluntary granularity

The information provided by configuration management tools is stored in a database of one form or another. Some configuration management tool sets come in a single program using a single-file database. Single-file database configuration management programs are usually found on mainframe computers. Single-file database structures frequently involve excessive computation or storage, which is not appropriate for networked environments.

In the local area network environment, it makes no sense to store a single-file database on the file server. Access to the single file becomes a bottleneck to effective and efficient work. A better solution is to have a multiple-file, or distributed database. The most popular and complete configuration management tools for network development on the market today support a distributed database.

One advantage to having a distributed database is that multiple levels of configuration information, each with a different granularity, may be stored. A database devoted strictly to release levels may reside alongside a database devoted to maintaining a complete module history. A database can be set up to track changes to all modules with many smaller subset databases set up to track each and every alteration of modules associated with different developers. No matter how the database is set up, the real advantage is that of freedom. No one method or capability is mandated by the tool set.

For example, a programming team may have one central database that provides tracking of all modules. Because nonrelevant revisions, such as a revision with a syntax error, are essentially useless revisions, many individually owned databases may be used to track intermediate changes on an individual basis. Every developer has access to a central archive that dynamically reflects changes to the modules that they are working on. When a developer needs to make a change, he or she acquires a working copy of the module from the central archive. The developer then checks the module into his or her individual workspace archive and begins the modification process. Changes are first stored in the developer's individual archive. If an error in code shows up due to a syntax error, the developer reedits the module and checks the repaired copy back into his or her individual archive and recompiles. This loop continues until compilation is successful. The latest revision from the individual workspace archive is then checked into the central archive. This methodology prevents the central archive from growing unnecessarily due to the storage of flawed modules. The disadvantage of this method is that the entire history of a module is not kept in a central place.

In another example, one database is devoted to tracking only release levels of the project. Perhaps this database is mirrored on a mainframe. Another database tracks every change, regardless of nature, for the development process. Once a version on the development database is released, the revisions associated with the released version are checked into the mainframe database.

In another example, one database tracks everything. Individual changes, test versions, custom versions, working versions, development versions, and release levels of the specifications, code, and documentation are maintained in this single database. Perhaps release levels are mirrored on the mainframe. Maybe only the current release is uploaded to the mainframe.

The Power of Perspective

Configuration management's ability to provide many perspectives of a project is very valuable. The user can obtain specific information and selectively ignore all other information. For example, the system integrator may need to know the revisions of each module that are associated with a given release. The system integrator does not care about the number of module revisions or why one module has more revisions than another. When quality assurance reports that the test version of the project is flawed, the developer who will fix the problems must be able to determine the exact revision level of the modules associated with the flawed test version.

Project management

Project managers need to be able to determine the state of the project at any given time. Using configuration management techniques and tools, it is easy to determine which parts of the project are currently under construction, are judged complete, are in test, and so on. The project manager can also examine and evaluate the project as a whole. Items like the current release level of the project or the number and names of custom alterations can readily be determined.

Promotion management

As a software system is developed, it goes through several stages in the software life cycle. Yet each individual module experiences its own growth which may spurt at times and lie dormant at others. Promotion management provides the capability to identify revision levels with a given promotion group, and to move the revision from one development stage, or promotion group, to the next. For example, promotion of a module from the development promotion group, DEV1, to the quality assurance promotion group, QA.

When a development version of the system is ready to be tested, it is promoted to the test version and, if promotion groups are used, to the test promotion group. When the test version has passed all tests and is ready for production, it is promoted to the production version. While there may be several steps along the way, configuration management tools should make the promotion process, sometimes called *phase transition*, a simple one.

Personnel management

Using configuration management tools and techniques, a manager can easily determine who is working on what modules. A simple command can inform the manager that one employee is working on three modules associated with the user interface and another employee is working on one module in the statistical analysis subsystem.

By changing a command parameter, a manager can generate and refine a report that provides specific information. Perhaps one developer has been working on a single module for an excessive period of time. The manager can identify the module, examine the change comments, and evaluate the performance of the developer. It may be that the developer is overloaded and needs help. It may be that the developer is in over his or her head in technical difficulty and needs assistance or training.

Security management

Each module of a system may have differing access requirements. For example, a module associated with the user documentation should not, in most cases, be edited by the engineering staff or even the document review staff. Developers should not edit specifications. Test engineers should not modify source code. Configuration management tools should provide the ability to determine the module access rights and privileges of each user or group of users on a case-by-case basis. Even within a single group, differing access rights and privileges are necessary. Senior developers may need to be able to create new modules on the fly while junior developers may be strictly prohibited from the same privilege.

Engineering management

Configuration management can be an effective engineering management tool. By producing accurate reports, engineering managers can determine the current status and progress of the project. Subsystems can be examined. Work flow can be charted. Problems can be identified before they impact the schedule or cause a major redesign of a system or subsystem. Using configuration management tools and techniques helps reduce the "nasty surprise" scenario.

System management

Configuration management use can also benefit the management and development of the system itself. Consider the following example:

> A subsystem was compiled and tested on Friday of last week and found to work as defined. The subsystem code has been modified since last

Friday as development work on the project continues. Today the subsystem was recompiled and retested. The new version of the subsystem fails to run.

What change caused the failure? Was it the change itself or a reaction to the change that caused the failure? Using configuration management tools, the changed modules can be identified within minutes. The exact changes to all affected modules of the subsystem can be generated in one or more reports and the changes can then be examined and evaluated. In most cases, the newly introduced bug can be readily determined and repaired. In the exceptional cases where there is still not enough information to determine the cause of the failure, an impact document can be produced to find the names of the modules that call on or are called by the changed modules. Using a configuration management system, bug tracking becomes a methodical approach rather than a disorganized hunt.

Prior to the implementation of configuration management, a bug hunt for a newly introduced bug could take several person weeks of effort, if not months. With the implementation of configuration management, tracking down the newly introduced bug can usually be accomplished in minutes.

Summary

Configuration management is implemented with a variety of tools that provide information about any and all aspects of a software project; from personnel data to the smallest change in the smallest module. All phases and parts of the project that are subject to change should be maintained in the configuration management domain.

Each user of the configuration management system can obtain relevant information about the project or private code. Configuration management provides a dynamic global perspective of the software life cycle of one or more software systems.

Questions

1. Often, a bug in a software system will be repaired only to reappear at a later date. Explain how and why the use of configuration management techniques prevents the reintroduction of bugs that have already been repaired.

2. In many organizations, the evaluation department and the development department scorn each other. Why does this common scenario develop? How can configuration management techniques be used to prevent or eliminate the evaluation versus development attitude problem?

3

Implementing Configuration Management

The Configuration Management Tool Set

There are several tools that need to be integrated in order to implement a complete configuration management environment. The tools may be provided in a single application program or may be distributed across several application programs. Regardless of whether you construct your own tool set or buy a commercial package, several tools are required; a document change manager, a version manager, a release manager, a construction manager, a report generator, and a relationship detector. In the mainframe development arena, or when multiple development sites are employed, a communications manager is also an important tool.

Document change manager

Document change management is the key ingredient in the configuration management recipe. This tool maintains a record of all changes (called *deltas*) to all modules in the form of revisions. In the ideal situation, the change management tool should be able to track versions and releases.

An important consideration when evaluating change managers is the method employed to store changes. Originally, change managers stored the very first revision whole and complete. As new revisions were added, the change information measuring from the last stored module were added to the database. This is called *forward delta storage* (refer to Fig. 3.1). The problem with forward delta storage is that as more revisions are added, more computation is required to obtain the latest revision. The forward delta change manager must always start with the very first revision and then apply the deltas one at a time to

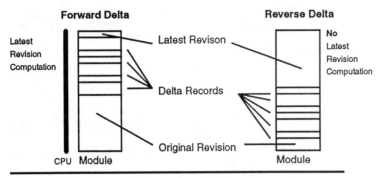

Figure 3.1   Delta (change) storage in a database file.

create the latest revision. The problem is further exacerbated when a new revision is checked in. Again, the change manager must start at the original revision and apply the deltas one at a time until the latest revision is constructed. Once this has been accomplished, the last stored revision is compared to the revision being checked in and a new delta record is generated and appended to the file. As more revisions are added to the file, the longer each operation takes. Note the CPU bar next to the forward delta module file in Fig. 3.1. The CPU bar represents computational requirements.

More recent change manager programs take a different and more efficient approach, called *reverse delta storage*. In reverse delta storage, only the most recent revision of the module is kept whole and complete. When a new revision is checked in, the new revision is compared to the last revision and no computation of the latest revision is required. A new delta record is computed and added to the file and the complete new revision is stored. The advantage of reverse delta storage is that of performance. No computation is required to determine the latest revision. In Fig. 3.1, there is no CPU computation bar next to the reverse delta module. The performance issue is especially important when you realize that over 85 percent of all archive accesses are for the latest revision.

Why is reverse delta storage better than forward delta storage? How many times is the latest revision of a module accessed? How many times is an older revision accessed? The older the revision, the less apt it is to be accessed. What happens when many revisions are stored? With forward delta storage, it takes a long time to check out the latest revision. With reverse delta storage, no computation is required, you get a copy of the latest revision as fast as the machine can provide it.

When a change is entered, the tool should store only the information it needs to recreate the previous revision of the module. When this is the case, storage requirements are minimized and performance is optimized.

The change manager should also store additional information about the module and changes to it. Storing just the changes provides useful but limited information. The change manager should note the date stamp associated with the file, and therefore its last modification time, when it is checked in as well as the time and date when the file was actually checked in. The author's name should also be stored. A good change manager will request a module description when a new module is first checked in and request the author's comments when a new revision is checked in. The additional information and descriptive comments should be stored along with the delta information. An excellent change management system will also provide a mechanism by which the author's change comments may be stored in the module itself in the form of a comment block.

Version manager

A version manager is an integral part of the change management system. The change manager and the version manager must be integrated. Typically, both the version manager and the change manager are part of the same program or program set.

Where the change manager manages revisions of individual modules, the version manager tracks versions of a system. This is usually accomplished with a version label. A version label is a text string that is attached to a specific revision identifying that revision as a member of the version. A version label may indicate only one revision of a module whereas a single revision of a module may contain many version labels.

A simple system consisting of four modules is illustrated in Fig. 3.2. Module A experienced one change before the alpha version label was assigned to it. A modification was made to module A because of a bug in the alpha version. A new revision was checked in prior to the beta version label assignment. A bug in the beta version resulted in yet

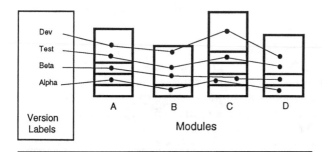

Figure 3.2   Version tracking with version labels.

another revision. The latest revision is part of the test version which has been unchanged since the test version label was assigned. Testing has not uncovered any new bugs, therefore the latest revision is also a part of the development version.

Module B experienced one change since the alpha version label was assigned due to a discovered bug. Since the beta version, no bugs have been discovered and the module remains unchanged. The latest revision of module B is associated with the beta, test and development versions.

Module C experienced a change after the beta label was assigned when a bug was found by a beta site and subsequently fixed by development. The fixed revision is now in the test version. Testing discovered that the bug was not completely eradicated, therefore a newer revision with the enhanced repair is in the development version. It will not be tested until the next iteration of the test process, that is, when the development version is promoted to test.

A bug was discovered in the alpha version of module D and repaired for the Beta version. While in beta test, a new bug was discovered and repaired. The repaired version is currently in test and no new bugs have been discovered. The latest revision is a member of both the test and development versions.

When the versions of a product are identified, it becomes a simple task to reconstruct any prior version of the product.

Release manager

A release of a product is constructed from a specific set of revisions. A release is really another form of a version. Releases, like versions, are tracked with version labels. Because a version label is simply a string of text, the version label can identify anything desired. One version label may identify a specific release, for example, *Release 1.0*, while another version label may be used to identify a custom release, such as *Release 1.0 for ABC Banking, Inc.* Any good version manager product should be able to maintain release level tracking. Note that revision numbers are distinct from release numbers. Release 1.0 of a product may not even have a single module of revision 1.0.

System construction manager

A system construction manager program is a program that automates the system build process. Many programmers are familiar with a program called *make* which is a simple-minded construction manager. The construction manager program reads a file, sometimes called a *makefile* or *build script*, and evaluates the ingredients of the program. Rules are also evaluated. For example, when a source code file, called a *dependent*, is compiled, it creates an object file, called a *target*. The object file is built from the source code file. A target is built from its dependencies. If a source code module is more recent than its object file target, the target is out of date. The date stamps of dependent files are checked against the date stamps of the targets to see if any portion of the system is out of date. Any source files that are of more recent vintage than the corresponding target files are processed to produce an up-to-date target file.

The primary purpose of the system construction manager is to eliminate human errors when constructing the system. The system architecture needs to be defined in a build script. The system definition consists of a listing of dependencies and targets. Note that a target can have more than one dependent. For example, the executable program produced may have several object files and libraries as dependencies.

Most make programs are simple-minded. Every single step that the program is to take must be spelled out in the makefile. The more sophisticated construction managers are rule-based and provide on-the-fly decision-making capabilities. The ability to make decisions, interpret macros, and perform actions based upon rules and circumstances provides significant power to a build manager.

Report generator

While revision, version, and release management are critical tasks in the configuration management domain, there needs to be a way to obtain the information contained in the various managers. A user should be able to obtain specific information upon request.

Many configuration management programs tout their fancy formatted reports. However, keep in mind that form is not nearly as important as content. Once data has been generated in any format, it can be reformatted either through an automatic filter or by hand. It is much more important to obtain raw critical information than to produce a vague but pretty report. Content is more important than appearance. However, appearance does help. A report builder that provides complete information and allows the user to specify the format of the report offers the best of both worlds.

Reports take many forms. A programmer may need to find out the exact difference between two revisions of a module. The programmer really doesn't care if the format of the report is pretty. It is very important to the programmer that the report be accurate and readable. A manager may need to determine which modules are currently under edit. The manager may like to see pretty reports, but is more interested in the content of the report. A short listing of all locked modules with the names of the lock owners and dates of the lock actions is sufficient to the manager's needs.

This is not to say that a configuration management program that produces pretty reports generates meaningless pretty reports. Many configuration management programs with report formatting provide very good information. But you should choose functionality over fancy. Many programs exist that can format a report. An experienced programmer can easily construct a custom program with off-the-shelf programming languages or tools.

Relations detection

There are two primary relations reports that are of significant value in the configuration management arena. The first is the *where used document*. The second is the *data impact statement*. Both of these relations reports are very similar in nature. These reports are generated through a process called *impact analysis*.

The where used document lists all program modules by name. Associated with each module is a list that contains the name of any other module that "calls" the module in question. The data impact statement lists all data types. Every module that references a data type is listed under the data type name. By using the where used document, a user can quickly determine where each module is used in the system. The user can also determine which modules may be impacted by a change in any other module. By using the data impact statement, a user can quickly determine which modules will be affected if a specific data type is altered.

If a programmer needs to alter a module for some reason, the where used document tells the programmer what other modules may need modification to reflect the changes made to the altered module. For example, if a new calling parameter is added to the module definition, every other module that calls the altered module must be updated to reflect the new calling parameter.

If the design engineer determines that specification for one data type used in the program needs to be changed, the engineer can use the data impact statement to determine which modules may be impacted by the proposed change. The modules can then be evaluated in light of the proposed change for potential impact.

Communications manager

A communications manager manages communications between two or more computer systems. There are two circumstances in which a communications manager becomes an important tool. If mainframe development has been off-loaded to a network of personal computer workstations, the production version of the system must be uploaded to the mainframe upon which it will run. The new production version must not only run on the mainframe, it should also be stored in the mainframe's version control system. Storing the new production version along with the prior production version provides an easy and fast recovery if the new production version contains a bug or fatal flaw.

The other circumstance where communications management becomes important is when more than one site is using or developing the same source code. When a site needs to be updated, the communications manager should transmit the deltas to the site instead of a whole new listing. Transmitting only deltas speeds up the transmission process. The receiving site then uses the communications manager to update the source as required.

Choosing the Tool Set

A number of commercial configuration management products are available on the market today. Some implement all configuration management functions within a single program. Some distribute the functionality through several programs. In general, networked workstations download applications from the file server. The larger the application, the longer the download takes. In addition, most networked personal computer workstations have a limited memory capability. Large programs must use functional overlays which reside in memory. However, only one overlay at a time can be active. Why take the time to download executable code that is not needed for a given function? Not only is a distributed database a good construct, so is a distributed functionality.

Another important factor is ease of use. Is the product so complicated that programmers will shy away from using it? What good is a tool if it is not used correctly? The more complicated the user interface, the longer it takes to learn to use the product. The harder it is to use the product, the harder it is to get everyone to use it. Ideally, the tool set should be easy to learn and use.

Finally, ease of use is one thing, but functionality is another. If the product is easy to learn and use but does not do the job expected, the product is a waste of time and money. A balance must be achieved.

The Available Tools

Perhaps the best product is one in which the complexity of functionality is available yet the individual use is easy. A vast functionality exists but each user only accesses the portion that is of relevance. Both database and functionality are distributed. INTERSOLV's PVCS Configuration Management Series of products is perhaps the best configuration management tool set on the market today. This product series provides configuration management tools for stand-alone personal computers, networked workstations, and mainframe as host for stand-alone workstations or networked workstations environments. Because of the excellent job put into this product line, INTERSOLV enjoys the vast market share in the personal computer and networked DOS and OS/2 workstation arena.

Document change: PVCS version manager

The PVCS Version Manager uses reverse deltas to maximize performance and provides revision, version, release, and security managers in a single package consisting of a number of small executable programs. The product can store any kind of file, binary or text. The product supports branching and merging, fixed and floating version labels, and can generate many reports. The product also supports optional data compression to save disk space.

Included within the PVCS Version Manager is functionality that provides a mechanism by which off-site source users can be updated with deltas instead of complete source. The receiving site can than use the PVCS Version Manager to update source code and other files to current levels.

System construction:
PVCS configuration builder

The PVCS Configuration Builder is a rule based program with macros, loops, conditional constructs, and on-the-fly decision capabilities. Rules are embedded within the program but may be redefined in a global context to enhance or customize their operation in any environment. The user may also define rules that are specific to a particular system in the system's build script. There are several types of macros including predefined, automatically-defined and user-defined. Defining macros is easy and a very powerful feature. Because it is rule-based, build scripts are easier to produce and maintain. The product generates a true minimal build path to maximize performance and minimize the work required to generate a system. The product can also automatically generate dependency listings which makes the generation of build scripts a trivial task. The PVCS Configuration Builder is basically a very much improved make program.

Report generation: PVCS reporter

New to the PVCS Configuration Management Series of products is the PVCS Reporter. The PVCS Reporter generates change history reports.

A number of report types come as defaults with the product. The user can easily define and save custom reports as well. With the PVCS Reporter, it is easy to format attractive reports that contain complete and useful information.

Communications manager:
PVCS production gateway

The PVCS Production Gateway product provides the ability to synchronize networked development with mainframe library systems. The product supports a variety of mainframe library systems.

Relation detection

Only one tool remains to be provided, the relationship detector. A relationship detector is that tool that provides the where used document. The relationship detector may also provide a data impact statement. Unfortunately, no good relation detection product is on the market today. However, it can be expected that this hole in the configuration management scenario will soon be filled by INTERSOLV.

A where used document is a very important tool. Generally, source code files are text files. Other types of files are accessed by an application, such as binary graphics images, and so on. These other types of files are not interrelated as is source code. A source code module may call other source code modules. In fact, it is very rare that a source code module makes only library function calls. Most every source code module calls one or more functions or procedures contained in other source code modules.

A Tool to Build the Missing Tool

Because source code files are textual in nature. A text and file processing language would be the best to use to provide the relationship detector. No organization or person wants to spend a lot of time generating a program to produce the relationship detector. A fast and easy to use language with file and text sorting capabilities built in is the ideal tool to produce the relations detector with a minimum of effort and time.

One such language is the AWK programming language. AWK was originally designed under the UNIX operating system to provide a fast and efficient method of changing data formats, validity checking, searching, and printing reports. AWK is very powerful and easy to use. A one line AWK program may be equivalent to a fifty line program written in another language such as C, BASIC or COBOL. AWK works with pattern-action pairs with file handling and text comparison routines built into the language. For example, a program written in AWK to print a file to the display screen consists of one short line of code: "{print}".

Portability issues

The AWK language is portable without change across a variety of platforms. Almost every UNIX machine has AWK provided as part of the operating system tool set. AWK is also available for DOS and OS/2 platforms. Normally, AWK is an interpreted language, that is, the code is processed by an interpreter at run time. This is a slow process as anyone who has worked with interpreted BASIC can verify.

Perhaps the best implementation of AWK for DOS and OS/2 is provided by Thompson Automation. The product has a unique advantage in that it provides an AWK compiler. An AWK program can be compiled into a stand-alone executable. The Thompson Automation AWK product was formerly known as PolyAWK, and was sold by the same folks who created the PVCS Configuration Management Series.

Programming issues

While AWK is easy to use, some of the constructs are not so easy to understand. AWK uses a pattern matching format called *regular expressions* which also originated with the UNIX operating system. Even though regular expressions are cryptic, they are very powerful. It is regular expressions that would be used to generate the where used document and the data impact statement.

The Thompson Automation AWK product provides a variety of tools and scripts including an easy-to-generate user interface. In less than 50 lines of AWK, a full-color, menu-driven user interface can be created.

Producing a where-used-document generator using AWK will not be a trivial task, but neither will it be overly difficult. In fact, by the time these words go to print, Thompson Automation may already have a where-used-document generator on the market.

Summary

The PVCS Configuration Management tool set is perhaps the best available on the market today. It is fully functional and provides all the tools necessary with the exception of impact analysis. It is fully expected that INTERSOLV will have an impact analysis tool on the market by the time you have this book in hand.

Questions

1. Why is it important to have tools that are integrated?

2. Would it not be better to find the best of each tool and use it regardless of who made it?

3. Can you effectively mix and match tools?

4. Is it really worth the time to learn a new language or tool set in order to implement configuration management?

5. What would happen if only a portion of the tools were implemented?

6. If only some tools were to be made available and you had to select which ones, which ones would you select?

4

Fundamentals of
Group Management

Group Definition

In the software development arena, a group is a collection of people dedicated to a specific purpose. An example of a group is a collection of programmers whose goal is to produce the code for an application program. A group is basically a subset of the team. The team is responsible for producing the complete product and may consist of a number of groups: the developers, the testers, the integrators, the documentation writers, and so on. Groups are differentiated by the tasks that its members perform. In a very large organization, first-line managers may also be organized into a group of their own.

The composition of a group is variable. A development group may consist of two or three senior programmers, four junior programmers and two entry-level programmers. Another development group may consist solely of a number of senior engineers or developers.

Group Responsibilities

Not only are groups defined by goal or task, but also by responsibility. A development group is responsible for the development of a system. The quality assurance group is responsible for the accuracy of the system and compliance of the application to the specification. The quality control group may be responsible for insuring compatibility with other applications and with the documentation. The documentation group is responsible for producing the user, installation, and maintenance documentation. Each group has a different set of responsibilities and tasks. Each group uses a different set of tools to accomplish its tasks. Programmers use compilers, writers use word processors, managers and team leaders use project managers. Groups also share a common subset of tools. Each group should use the exact same configuration management tool set as every other group, thus providing consistency from group to group.

Group Relationships

One of the biggest problems encountered in software development organizations is intergroup relations. Often times, the development group will complain about the quality assurance group and vice versa. Why is this so common? Could configuration management techniques reduce or remove the intergroup hostility? Yes. To see how configuration management techniques reduce the adversity between two groups, an understanding of some groups dynamics is necessary.

The ancient war

In many organizations, a conceptual division exists between development and testing groups. Sometimes, this division breaks out into open hostility. There is no valid reason for this war to continue, much less exist. Development and testing groups have a common goal. They both want to have a good product go out the door on time. They want to come in ahead of schedule and reap rewards for doing so. Unfortunately, their enthusiasm to do so is often times their undoing.

Usually, when development reaches a stage where the system is ready for test, a copy of the application or system is delivered to the care of the testing group. The testing group tests the product and discovers bugs, which are reported back to the development group. The development group repairs the bugs. This is the normal flow of the development process and also is how it should be. However, it is also during this process that problems can arise. One of the biggest problems is that the testing methodology for repaired bugs in previously tested code is often the cause of more bugs and other problems that cannot be readily tracked. The problem becomes clear when the testing process is evaluated.

Usually, testing an application is not a simple one or two day task. A very large and complicated application may take several months to test accurately. Fixes to bugs that were found during the test process are usually available for retest prior to completion of the test suite. Due to scheduling pressures, the bug fixes are normally folded into the version of the application under test. Some regression tests are performed to insure that the identified bug was fixed, and then testing resumes where it left off. How will the test group know if bugs that are discovered later in the test procedure were there when testing began? How will they know whether the bug was there originally or was newly introduced by one of the folded-in bug fixes?

They won't.

What happens if the bug fix breaks a section of the program that has already passed all of its tests? If this is the final round of testing before the product hits the streets, how will they know with any degree of confidence that the product really works as advertised?

They won't know.

Unfortunately, a large percentage of the time, some bug will not be discovered until the product has shipped. Most likely, it will be discovered by an irate customer.

When customer support reports the undiscovered bug, everyone gets excited. Development points their finger at test and says "You dummies!" Test points their finger at development and says "You dummies!"

Who is right? Is anybody right?

Peace at last

The solution to the problem is configuration management. When development has the system ready for test, The current revision levels which represent the system are labeled *development* by default. This is the development version. These revisions are all relabeled as *test* with a version label, creating the test version. The test version is used exclusively in the testing procedure. Bugs are reported and repaired as before. The difference is that the repaired bugs are not folded into the test version. The repaired code is in revisions that are *above* the test version. The test version remains unchanged until all testing has been completed. Any bugs found during the test process are existing bugs and have not been introduced as a result of a bug fix. The test version is a known entity, not a moving target. Once testing has been completed and all found bugs reported, the development group can prepare a new test version. Some time should elapse between completion of the test suites and generation of the new version. All reported bugs should either be fixed or addressed and deferred. Once all the bugs that are going to be fixed have been fixed, a new test version is generated. Any bug found when testing the new test version can be readily identified as either a bug that was not fixed or a bug that was introduced by another bug fix. The nature of the bugs is known! When the final round of testing is completed, the testing group can say with confidence that the product conforms to all specifications and contains no nasty surprises. All remaining bugs are known and identified! All remaining bug fixes have been postponed as minor irritants or deferred as future enhancements.

Group Access Rights

Each group, development, documentation, quality assurance, and others, has a different set of access needs. The development group needs to be able to access and modify source code files. The development group may also need to access specification and requirements files without the right to modify them. The documentation group must be able to access specification, source, and requirements files and to access and modify documentation files. The test group needs to access and modify test program source code files, test data files, and other testing related files.

Along with the need to access files of different types, different groups should be denied rights to other types of files. The test group should not be allowed to modify source code or documentation files. The documentation group should not be allowed to modify source code, test, or requirements files.

Each group should have its own set of access rights and privileges, as well as restrictions. Each group should be enabled to complete their assigned tasks without adverse impact from other groups and without impacting other groups adversely. The definition of group privileges and restrictions differs from one organization to another based upon the differing needs of the organization. Group privileges and restrictions for similar groups within an organization may differ due to the composition of the groups.

In general, there are seven groups that are associated with a software development organization. These groups are management, design, development, test, documentation, integration, and production. Some personnel may serve in multiple capacities, in which case they would be members of more than one group.

The management group

The *management group* consists of personnel managers who are not concerned with the actual content of files, but rather with their production and quality. The management group needs to be able to generate reports about the current status of the project. The management group also needs to be able to find out who is doing what to which files and how long have they been doing it.

For example, if a programmer has been working on a given module for several weeks, perhaps the programmer is in need of some assistance. Perhaps the module specification is too broad. Perhaps the module is particularly difficult to implement. Perhaps the programmer has been working on other projects to the detriment of the development of the module.

The management group has no business modifying specifications, requirements, source code, documentation, tests, or test data. Members of the management group may wish to access one or more of these file types to monitor the development of the files.

The design group

The *design group* is responsible for the implementation of specifications and requirements documents. Members of this group need to be able to access and modify specifications and requirements but do not need to be able to modify source code. If a designer is also a developer, perhaps he or she should belong to two groups, such as design and development. Members of the design group may wish to access source code and testing files to insure complicity with the requirements and specifications, but, in general, do not modify these file types.

The development group

Members of the *development group* access the specifications and requirements files to learn and understand what it is that they are to develop and to insure that what they have developed complies with the specifications and requirements thereof. The development group must be able to create and modify the source code files from which the target system is developed. The development group may find test programs and data of interest, but do not modify such files.

In many organizations, there is more than one development group. Each of these development groups may need to access the files of other development groups for informational purposes, but should not be allowed to modify the files that are being developed by a different development group.

The test group

The *test group*, whether it is called quality assurance or quality control, must be able to access and modify test programs and data. In some institutions the test group also must be able to access source code to build the test version of the product. In addition, the test group needs to access the documentation to ensure that the documentation reflects accurately the functionality and features of the product. The test group also needs to access specifications and requirements files to insure that the program actually meets the specifications and complies with the requirements.

The documentation group

The *documentation group* must be able to access requirements and specifications in order to write accurate user, maintenance, and other document and manual types. The documentation group has no need to access testing programs or test data unless information regarding these subjects is required in a given manual or document. The documentation group may need to access source code but only to the extent that they can accurately document the use or implementation of a given feature.

A subset of the documentation group is the *marketing group* that produces marketing information such as press releases, catalogues, brochures, and data sheets. The marketing group may use the specification definitions in the design phase of the product. However, once the specifications and requirements have been defined, the marketing group should have no modification rights to these type files. Their natural tendency is to want to modify the specifications and requirement over time to include perceived needs in the marketplace. This process must be monitored very closely because it is very hard for a development team to produce a product for a specification that is constantly shifting. Any and all modifications to specifications or requirements documents should be implemented by the design group, and only after serious consideration of the impact such changes would have on the development, testing, documentation, and integration groups.

The integration group

The *integration group* insures that multiple systems produced by a single organization all work together in peace and harmony. Not every organization needs to have an integration group, but where multiple related products are produced by a single organization, an integration group is essential.

The integration group needs to be able to access documentation and program files to ensure that consistency between product lines is achieved and maintained. The products must work together with as near to a common interface as is possible. One program product must not be allowed to damage the integrity or usefulness of another program product.

The production group

The *production group* is responsible for producing quantities of the finished product and the packaging and distribution thereof. The production group needs to be able to access the current production release of the software and associated documentation. The production group should not be allowed to modify any files of any types related to the specification, development, or testing of the product.

Group Member Access Rights

Not all members of a single group will have the same degree of experience or expertise. For example, a development group may consist of several entry-level programmers, several junior-level programmers, one or more senior programmers, and perhaps a project leader or principal engineer. The abilities and talents of each of the members at the same status, for example, entry-level, will probably differ as well. Also the personalities of the group members will be diverse.

Each level of individual group membership may require the establishment of different access rights and privileges, each geared specifically for that level. An entry-level programmer should probably not have the same privileges as a senior-level engineer. Perhaps an entry-level person who has been on the job just a few weeks should not have the same privileges as an entry-level person with several months on the job.

Another factor to consider is personality. Some people work well in team environments while others prefer solitude. Some people are not good at certain phases or portions of their jobs, such as commenting, while others are wonderful. Some high-level people who perform coding miracles may need to have several lower-level people follow after them to "clean up their messes." Some people feel that they should have the right to modify any other persons work because they think that they are better or more efficient than other team members. It is a real nightmare to find that something you have worked long and hard on has been modified without comment by someone else and you cannot even determine who did it. Imagine how you would feel if you spend several months perfecting a module only to have it destroyed in a single night by a wild-card team member who has left you with no record of the changes he or she made.

Simplification of Group Management

To simplify group management, the first thing to accomplish is a definition of the rights, responsibilities, and tasks of each group. When a group is so defined, there is no question about who can do what to which file type. Each group has a well-defined environment and task list that limits, yet directs, the efforts of the group. Less time is wasted by the group in nongroup tasks. Test does not fix code. Documentation does not modify code or specification to match documentation. Development does not modify specification to match code. Each group knows its tasks as responsibilities and devotes all of its time to accomplishing its own set of goals regardless of what any other group is doing.

Group needs, privileges, and restrictions

It is management's job to ensure that all obstacles to attaining goals are either removed or minimized. Once the tasks and responsibilities of a group have been defined, the needs of the group should be defined. Defining the needs of the group establishes the basic environment for the group.

Once the basic needs of a group are established, the next thing to evaluate is those items or privileges that will enable the group to better accomplish the group goals. The informational needs of the group must be evaluated. The types of information that will allow the group to produce better results must be defined. The ability of the group, as a whole, to modify the information must be determined.

Finally, an evaluation of the tasks or access rights that may hinder the attainment of group goals or will hinder or harm another group must be made. Any activity that will present an obstacle to the attainment of goals should be restricted or prohibited. Any activity that will harm the quality or schedule of another group's goals or tasks should be restricted or prohibited.

Identifying the group's many faces

When a definition of the group's tasks, privileges, and restrictions has been established, the group as a whole is defined. However, upon further analysis, it is often found that there is a diversity of tasks and responsibilities within the group. Some tasks and responsibilities are more suited for some group members than for others. The group itself may be divided into several subgroups, each with a different set of goals, tasks and responsibilities.

Summary

The production of a software product is a complicated procedure that requires many different talents and responsibilities. These responsibilities can be well defined and divided amongst team members forming groups. Each defined group has a given set of tasks, goals, responsibilities, rights, privileges, and restrictions. Each group member has his or her tasks, responsibilities, rights, privileges, and restrictions defined as well. Everyone knows what they are supposed to be doing and how they are supposed to do it. By producing a group definition, it becomes easy for management and team members to monitor the progress made by the team. By defining individual tasks, rights, responsibilities, and the like, it becomes easier for a manager to define objectives for each team member and then track the progress of the team member toward those goals. *Management by Objectives* (MBO) is greatly simplified as is the management of the group and its individual members.

Questions

1. Explain some of the consequences that an organization might face if members of the quality assurance team were allowed to modify source code to fix detected program errors.

2. The marketing arm of a company is supposed to have its fingers on the pulse of the customer. What harm could come if a project that is to take one year to implement has a new set of user specifications introduced in the third month of development? What if the new specifications were to arrive just after the design process completed?

3. If a team of programmers is supplemented by contract programmers, should the contract programmers belong to the same group as the employee programmers? Should they have the same rights and privileges? Should they have the same restrictions? Should employee and contract programmers belong to two distinct groups? Why or why not?

5

Implementing Security

Defining and implementing security is a relatively easy task if all actions possible in the development arena are broken down into a series of atomic actions. If each atomic action has an associated privilege and restriction, then each action can then be controlled on an individual basis. The atomic actions are then combined to produce overall privileges and restrictions. The PVCS tool set provides such atomic actions.

Once privileges and restrictions are defined, they need to be implemented in a secure fashion so that they cannot be modified by the users. As the project changes, new members are brought on board, other members leave, member responsibilities change, and so on, the security system must change to track those changes. The PVCS tool set provides mechanisms and tools to manage and maintain the security system.

Privileges and Restrictions

There are many actions that occur in the configuration management environment. Files are checked out for browsing purposes or for editing. Versions of a system or subsystem are defined. Revisions are added or deleted. The list of potential actions goes on and on and are accomplished by members of the product team. Each person associated with a project has different needs according to the group to which they belong, their talents, experience, and inclinations.

In order to construct a listing of the rights, privileges, and restrictions assigned to any user or group, a method that provides an easy to use mechanism by which such definitions may be accomplished must be established.

Base privileges and restrictions

A base privilege or restriction defines a single action element of an operation. For example, if a programmer wishes to check out the latest revision of a module for editing, several base actions occur. The user is getting a copy of the latest revision. The latest revision is usually the tip of the revision trunk. Therefore, the base action is getting a copy of the tip revision. The second base action is locking the retrieved revision with the programmer's name.

Each base action has an associated privilege as is illustrated in Table 5.1. The base privileges in this table provide a privilege definition for

TABLE 5.1   Base Privileges

Privilege	Allows user to:
AddVersion	add a version label
BreakLock	break another user's lock
ChangeAccessList	change an archive file's access list
ChangeCommentDelimiter	change an archive file's comment delimiter
ChangeOwner	change an archive file's owner's name.
ChangeProtection	change an archive file's protection attributes
ChangeWorkfileName	change the name of the archive file produced workfile.
DeleteRevNonTip	delete an older revision
DeleteRevTip	delete a tip revision.
DeleteVersion	delete a version label
GetNonTip	obtain a copy of an older revision
GetTip	obtain a copy of the latest revision
InitArchive	create a new archive file.
LockNonTip	lock an older revision
LockTip	lock the tip revision
ModifyWorkfileDescription	modify the description of the workfile.
ModifyChangeDescription	change the description of a modification
ModifyVersion	alter a version label.
PutBranch	check a revision into a branch
PutTrunk	check in a mainline revision.
StartBranch	create a branch
Unlock	remove their lock from a revision
ViewAccessDB	view privilege, user, and group definitions
ViewArchiveHeader	view and generate archive file reports.
ViewArchiveRev	view and generate revision reports.

all atomic actions that may be involved in any given operation. For each privilege, there is an equal and opposite restriction, as shown in Table 5.2. Using base privileges and restrictions it is possible to precisely define the access rights and prohibitions for any single user or group. It is possible, but it can also be very awkward unless a methodology is employed in creating the definitions. One method that will greatly reduce the confusion is to use composite privileges and restrictions.

PVCS composite privileges and restrictions

To simplify the process of defining an access right, predefined composite privileges and restrictions are available. These composite defini-

TABLE 5.2 Privileges and Matching Restrictions

Privilege	Restriction
AddVersion	NoAddVersion
BreakLock	NoBreakLock
ChangeAccessList	NoChangeAccessList
ChangeCommentDelimiter	NoChangeCommentDelimiter
ChangeOwner	NoChangeOwner
ChangeProtection	NoChangeProtection
ChangeWorkfileName	NoChangeWorkfileName
DeleteRevNonTip	NoDeleteRevNonTip
DeleteRevTip	NoDeleteRevTip
DeleteVersion	NoDeleteVersion
GetNonTip	NoGetNonTip
GetTip	NoGetTip
InitArchive	NoInitArchive
LockNonTip	NoLockNonTip
LockTip	NoLockTip
ModifyWorkfileDescription	NoModifyWorkfileDescription
ModifyChangeDescription	NoModifyChangeDescription
ModifyVersion	NoModifyVersion
PutBranch	NoPutBranch
PutTrunk	NoPutTrunk
StartBranch	NoStartBranch
Unlock	NoUnlock
ViewAccessDB	NoViewAccessDB
ViewArchiveHeader	NoViewArchiveHeader
ViewArchiveRev	NoViewArchiveRev

tions group actions of similar type. For example, the PutTrunk and PutBranch privileges are combined into a single privilege, *Put*. A complete list of composite privileges is found in Table 5.3. Composite restrictions are the opposite of the privileges and can be found in Table 5.4.

In Table 5.3, the last two privileges are special privileges and deserve some explanation. The *unlimited privilege* provides the user with all possible privileges. The user can perform any operation to any archive file as long as the user either owns the archive file or has legal access to the archive file. The *superuser privilege* has no such access restrictions. A user with the SuperUser privilege can perform any operation to any archive file regardless of ownership or access right. The superuser privilege is one that should be parceled out very carefully. Most organizations choose not to implement this privilege level because it wields too much power and the potential for human error is too great.

User-defined privileges and restrictions

The PVCS Version Manager product allows for creative permission and restriction definition. Actions for a particular operation or need can be analyzed and a user-defined access right defined. For example, the action of editing a revision consists of three atomic actions, *get*, *lock* and *put*. To further simplify creating large access right definitions,

TABLE 5.3   Predefined Composite Privileges

Privilege	Components
DeleteRev	DeleteRevTip & DeleteRevNonTip
Get	GetTip & GetNonTip
Lock	LockTip & LockNonTip
ModifyDescription	ModifyChangeDescription & ModifyWorkfileDescription
Put	PutBranch & PutTrunk
ViewArchive	ViewArchiveHeader & ViewArchiveRev
Unlimited	All privileges(must own or have legal access to archive file)
SuperUser	All privileges (no restrictions)

TABLE 5.4   Predefined Composite Restrictions

Restriction	Components
NoDeleteRev	NoDeleteRevTip & NoDeleteRevNonTip
NoGet	NoGetTip & NoGetNonTip
NoLock	NoLockTip & NoLockNonTip
NoModifyDescription	NoModifyChangeDescription & NoModifyWorkfileDescription
NoPut	NoPutBranch & NoPutTrunk
NoViewArchive	NoViewArchiveHeader & NoViewArchiveRev

such as for an entire group, small, similar action-oriented access rights can combined and a user-defined privileges and restrictions set be defined as a single-access right.

Some example definitions of action-oriented access rights are found in Table 5.5. Note that once a user-defined access right has been created, it may be used in the definition of further access rights. PVCS evaluates access right definitions in order. A user-defined access right must be defined before it can be used in another user-defined access right. While you can name an access right anything you want, if you use the name of an existing base or predefined access right, you may not use your new user-defined access right in another user-defined access right definition. In this case, the access right you are defining will use the original definition for the privilege set with a duplicated name. The safest and the easiest-to-read method is to assign unique names to user-defined access rights.

Refer again to Table 5.5. All but the last two access right definitions are action oriented. The last two definitions are user oriented. The first definition, *Creator*, allows a person to initialize new archive files, edit any revision in an archive file, and to create branches. The second definition, *SeniorEdit* allows a person to edit any revision or to create branches, but the definition does not allow the user to initialize a new archive file.

Once all possible relevant actions been defined, the various user-defined access rights can be combined into larger user-defined access rights. The large definitions can be applied to individuals and groups

TABLE 5.5 Example User-Defined Access Rights

User-defined access right	Components
FixComment	ModifyChangeDescription, NoModifyWorkfileDescription
Editor	FixComment, ViewArchive & NoInitArchive
EditTip	GetTip, LockTip, NoLockNonTip & Editor
EditTrunk	EditTip & PutTrunk
EditBranch	EditTip, PutBranch, NoStartBranch & Editor
CreateBranch	Get, Lock, Put, StartBranch & Editor
CreateFile	ModifyDescription & InitArchive
EditAll	Get, Lock, Put, StartBranch & ViewArchive
ViewTipRev	GetTip, NoLockTip
ViewPastRev	GetNonTip, NoLockNonTip
ViewAllRev	Get & NoLock
Creator	CreateFile & EditAll
SeniorEdit	EditAll & Editor

TABLE 5.6 Group Privilege Definitions

Group right	Composition
DevelopEdit	Creator
DevelopView	ViewAllRev
DocEdit	Creator
DocView	ViewAllRev
TestEdit	Creator
TestView	ViewAllRev
Mgmt	ViewArchive

as necessary. Group access rights are defined in Table 5.6. Note that each group has two definitions. The first definition enables members of the group to perform work. The second group definition allows members of the group to browse files. The reason each group has these two definitions is that while the group may need to work on some files, there may be other files that the group may need to browse but may not be allowed to edit. For example, the documentation group needs to be able to work on documentation files and may need to view, but not alter, specification or source code files. Another thing to note is that each group's working privilege definition must target the permissions needed by the most privileged member of that group.

Assigning a high level of permissions to a group does not necessarily provide all members of that group with the same permissions. A member of a group has his or her own permission definition, which limits that member to a specific set of access rights. While no group member may exceed the group access rights, the group access rights may exceed that of any one member. The rule of thumb is that when user and group access rights are combined, the greatest combined restriction is applied to the group member. Refer to Table 5.7. The group access right is Creator, which permits the greatest range of permissible actions. Member #1 of the group is the only person who has access to all actions permitted to the group and is the only member of the group who can create a new archive file. Member #2 has nearly the same privilege level, but cannot create new archive files. Member #3 can only perform those operations allowed by their permission. Member #3 cannot create archive files or branches and may not edit any branch revision.

To further clarify the greatest restriction paradigm, imagine that an access right definition is a binary word with one bit for each base permission. If the action is allowed, the bit is set to one. If the action is

TABLE 5.7 Group and Member Privilege Definitions

Who	Privilege
DevelopEdit	Creator
Member #1	Creator
Member #2	SeniorEdit
Member #3	EditTrunk
Member #4	EditTrunk
Member #5	CreateBranch
Member #6	EditTrunk & EditBranch
Member #7	EditBranch

TABLE 5.8   Group Member Computer Permission

Who	Permission Code
Group	1101100111011101
Member	0101010001001010
Net Member Permission	0101000001001000

not allowed, the bit is set to zero. The group permission in Table 5.8 contains actions not allowed in the member permission. The member permission contains actions not allowed in the group permission. To determine the actual permission permitted the group member, a logical AND operation is performed upon the group and member permissions. Even if the user has a privilege that the group does not have, that privilege will be denied in the final analysis. The action will be permitted only if the result of the logical AND operation has a one in the appropriate bit.

A group member's individual permission level may exceed that of the group. The member may belong to more than one group. One group may have permissions not allowed in another group, and the user may require those permissions as a member of the group with the greater permission level.

Implementing privileges and restrictions

When viewed as a whole, the actual assignment of permissions and restrictions appears rather complicated. However, when divide and conquer techniques are applied to the problem, the actual definition determination is relatively easy. To make it easy, construct a table, either by hand or in a spreadsheet. Each column of the table represents an atomic action. Use base privileges. When complete definition of atomic actions has been accomplished, create user-defined atomic permissions as in Table 5.5 to simplify the assignment process. The contents of the rows of the spreadsheet depend upon whether or not users or groups are being defined.

Defining Users

When defining user privilege levels, each row of the table will represent a user. Each user is evaluated by talent, assigned tasks, and experience. Fill in the table with check marks in each column that represents a permission. Once the table is completed, examine the table for commonalties. Use found commonalties to create atomic user-defined privileges as illustrated in Table 5.7.

Users are then assigned the maximum privilege that they will require to perform their assigned tasks and duties. Specific limitations for specific given tasks or needs are defined when the user is assigned membership in one or more groups.

Defining Groups

When defining groups, each row of the table represents a different set of files to which access is to be permitted. For example, row 1 may represent source code, row 2 specifications, row 3 documentation, row 4 test programs, and row 5 test data.

Fill in the table with check marks for each action allowed in each file type. Just as in the user definitions, look for commonalties and combine them. The result will be a listing of privileges. Using the above row definitions, perhaps two privilege levels will be required in the final analysis. This means that the group will have two group definitions. Perhaps "GroupEdit" and "GroupBrowse" permission definitions will suffice for the group.

Each group member is a member of both group definitions. If a member of the development group accesses a test program, he or she would do so as a member of "DevelopmentBrowse". Even if a development group member has Creator privileges in group "DevelopmentEdit", he or she would not have edit rights as a member of DevelopmentBrowse.

The Many-Talented Exception

Sometimes a single person has multiple responsibilities and talents and, therefore, performs multiple functions. In this case, the single person can be assigned membership in multiple groups. For example, a developer who is also a documentation writer may belong to four groups, "DevEdit", "DevBrowse", "DocEdit", and "DocBrowse". Another solution is to not assign such a person to any group. Instead, give that person unlimited or superuser status. The alternate solution may not be appropriate in large organizations and, in fact, may be a poor solution in that circumstance.

The AccessList

Once the access rights of individuals and groups have been defined, it is necessary to implement a method by which these access rights can be assigned to the various file types. Because the access rights may vary between file types, the only way to ensure complicity across file types is to store a list of those users and groups who have access rights to certain file types in the files themselves. This is accomplished by a archive file attribute called the *AccessList*. (Refer to Chap. 7 for further information about archive file attributes.)

Definition of the AccessList attribute

An AccessList is a listing of all groups and members that have access to a file. Each and every archive file has its own AccessList. When a file is accessed by a user, PVCS first obtains the user's name and then constructs a list of the groups to which the member belongs. The AccessList is then traversed to find a match between either a group or the user's name on the AccessList. If a match is found, the requested action is compared to the permissions listed for the matched access name. If the action is permitted, the action occurs and the list traversal terminates. If the action is not permitted, the AccessList traversal continues until either the action is permitted or the end of the AccessList is reached with no match.

For example, many-talented programmer "AUser" is a member of groups "AGroupEdit", "AGroupBrowse", "CGroupEdit", and "CGroup-Browse". AUser attempts to check out a file for edit whose AccessList consists of "AGroupBrowse, BGroupBrowse, CGroupEdit". When the AccessList is traversed, it is found that the user is a member of "AGroupBrowse" but has no edit rights under this group. No action occurs. The user is not a member of "BGroupBrowse". so again, no action occurs. Finally, the user is a member of "CGroupEdit" and as such has edit rights. AUser's command is honored and the edit permitted.

Constructing the AccessList

Each file type may have differing access rights for different groups. To determine what kind of file type access each group should have, construct a table or spreadsheet. The columns represent file types. The rows hold the various group names. Fill out the table as illustrated in Table 5.9, with yes or no values for each type of access for each type of file. When completed, it is a simple matter to determine which groups to include in each file type AccessList, as shown in Table 5.10.

Implementing the AccessList

By default, any newly created archive file inherits its AccessList from the PVCS configuration file's definition thereof. This default method does not work well when there are varying file types with different AccessLists. There are two ways to overcome this obstacle.

TABLE 5.9   AccessList Construction

Group	Specs	Source	Test	Testdata	Doc
Design	Yes	Yes	Yes	Yes	No
DevEdit	No	Yes	No	No	No
DevBrowse	Yes	No	No	No	Yes
TestEdit	No	No	Yes	Yes	No
TestBrowse	Yes	Yes	No	No	Yes
DocEdit	No	No	No	No	Yes
DocBrowse	Yes	Yes	No	No	No

The first method involves assigning access lists by hand. No default AccessList is defined in the configuration file. As each new archive file is created, the creator uses the administrative command "VCS -a" to assign an access list. If and only if the AutoCreate configuration parameter is in effect, the creator can assign an AccessList by using the "PUT -a" option. Both of these methods are cumbersome and prone to human error. Further, use of the AutoCreate configuration parameter is not recommended for team environments.

The recommended method extends the default assignment action by using a predefined set of users who can create archive files. Each user with creation privileges belongs to a specific group whose files have a specific AccessList requirement. A conditional construct in the configuration file sets the default AccessList parameter by determining the name of the user and setting the AccessList appropriately. An example of a conditional construct in the configuration file is illustrated in Fig. 5.1. This method automates the AccessList determination and assignment process.

TABLE 5.10   AccessList Assignment

File Type	Groups with access needs
Specs	Design,DevBrowse,TestBrowse, DocBrowse
Source	Design,DevEdit,TestBrowse, DocBrowse
Test	Design,TestEdit
TestData	Design,TestEdit
Doc	DevBrowse,TestBrowse,DocEdit

```
%if "$(VCSID)" == "User1"
      ACCESSLIST=Design,DevBrowse,TestBrowse,DocBrowse
%elseif "$(VCSID)" == "User2"
      ACCESSLIST=Design,DevEdit,TestBrowse,DocBrowse
%elseif "$(VCSID)" == "User3" || "$(VCSID)" == "User4"
      ACCESSLIST=Design,TestEdit
%elseif "$(VCSID)" == "User5"
      ACCESSLIST=DevBrowse,TestBrowse,DocEdit
%endif
```

Figure 5.1   AccessList assignment by conditional construct.

Managing the AccessList

The archive file AccessList can consist of group and user names. However, using the names of individual users can create management problems. If individual names are used, then each time a personnel change occurs, a name must be added or subtracted from the list. Adding a new name is easy with the administrative command "VCS -a *newuser.*" Removing a user name is not easy. The current AccessList must be deleted using "VCS -a" with no user or group names. Next, the new access list must be added using "VCS -a *newAccessList.*" The more names on the access list, the longer the command line to read the remaining users. This method is cumbersome at best and very prone to error.

The best method for managing the archive file access list is to use group names only. Perhaps, if a few users are unquestionably permanent team members who fall under the many-talented category, their names can be used. Using only group names means that as team members are added or leave the project, only the group membership definition need be redefined. The AccessList contained in the archive files does not need to be altered.

Implementing Security

There are two methods of implementing security. The size of an organization and the number of simultaneous projects determines the method used. Even if the organization is large, if only one project is active at a time, the simple method of implementing security is sufficient.

Regardless of the method selected, a text file containing all privilege, user, and group information must be constructed. The order of definitions should be privilege first, users second, and groups last. This text file will be used to construct an encoded binary file that is the access-control database. The text file should be stored in a location that no unauthorized personnel may access. Some organizations store this text file on a floppy disk and lock the floppy disk in a safe. It may also be a good idea to lock up a print out of the file, just in case.

The easiest way to implement security is to build a single access-control database. Each PVCS program has the name of the access-control database embedded into the program itself. When a user issues a PVCS command, the invoked program examines the access-control database and determines group membership, performs the AccessList traversal, and determines the net permissions of the user.

To implement the easy security method, use "VCONFIG", the install-time configuration program. First, "VCONFIG" tells all the PVCS applications that security is in use. This is accomplished by changing working directories to the directory in which PVCS was installed and running:

"VCONFIG -s *.exe"

The "VCONFIG" program will not alter non-PVCS applications.

Next, determine the location where the access-control database will be stored and give it a name. For example, the access-control database could be "SYS1:\admin\pvcs\access.db". With "VCONFIG". use the name and location of the access-control database to embed the name and location into all PVCS executable programs. The command to do so is:

"VCONFIG -a"SYS1:\admin\pvcs\access.db"

Optionally, both commands can be issued at once. For example:

"VCONFIG -s -a"SYS1:\admin\pvcs\access.db"

One of the PVCS programs which will be so configured is "MAKEDB". The "MAKEDB" program produces the encrypted database file from the input text file that contains the privilege, user, and group definitions. The "VCONFIG -a" program embeds the name of the encrypted file into the "MAKEDB" executable image. To produce the encrypted database file, simply execute "MAKEDB *inputfile*" where *inputfile* is the name of the definitions text file.

Multiple Security Levels

In some organizations, a single access-control database will not suffice. In this case, the configuration file variable "AccessDB" determines which access-control database will be used from one instance to another. A conditional construct contained in a configuration file provides the mechanism by which the dynamic decision of which access-control database file to use will be made. Using multiple access-control database files provides a mechanism by which each group manager can edit and maintain his or her own access-control database rather than having one person maintaining the database for the entire organization.

To implement the multiple access-control database environment, do not use the "VCONFIG" program to embed the access control database name. Instead, use only "VCONFIG -S" to turn security on and then use the AccessDB configuration parameter in a conditional construct in the Master Configuration File.

Multiple Project Security

One instance in which multiple access-control database files are a distinct advantage is when more than one project occurs simultaneously. In this case, the conditional construct can be implemented in a Master Configuration File. The conditional construct may dependent upon the user setting an environmental variable, for example, "PROJECT." The conditional construct should test for project definition and valid project names. The construct should return an error message if the project is undefined or is not valid. If the project is valid, then the "AccessDB" parameter can be set to indicate the name of an access-control database file to use for that project. An example configuration file conditional construct is illustrated in Fig. 5.2.

```
%if %defined $(PROJECT)

        %if  "$(PROJECT)"=="LAND"
             ACCESSDB=SYS1:\VCS\REAL.DB
        %elseif  "$(PROJECT)"=="BIGBUCKS"
             ACCESSDB=SYS1:\VCS\BALANCE.DB
        %elseif  "$(PROJECT)"=="LAYOUT"
             ACCESSDB=SYS1:\VCS\SPREAD.DB
        %else ECHO Invalid PROJECT defined
             ECHO Use DOS SET command to repair
             ABORT
        %endif
        DISALLOW AccessDB

%else ECHO    PROJECT not defined
      ECHO    Use DOS SET command
      ECHO    Valid projects:
      ECHO            LAND
      ECHO            BIGBUCKS
      ECHO            LAYOUT
      ECHO    Example:
      ECHO            SET PROJECT=BIGBUCKS
      ABORT
%endif
```

Figure 5.2   Example "PROJECT" conditional construct.

The AccessDB parameter should only be set in the Master Configuration File. Once the parameter AccessDB is set in the Master Configuration File, it must be disallowed using the "Disallow" configuration parameter. This prevents any user from redefining the AccessDB parameter and defeating the established security.

Maintaining Security

Maintenance of security is greatly simplified if the archive file AccessList consists of group names only. While one or two key personnel may have their individual names in the AccessList, a change of project, job, or any other change to one of these key people would mean that the AccessList of each and every archive file would need to be edited. If, on the other hand, all personnel are members of groups, and only groups may access the archive files, the maintenance of the AccessList in each archive file goes away!

When only groups can access archive files, then the individual membership and their permission levels are easily maintained by simply editing a text file. The text file, as described above, is used as input to the program "MAKEDB", which produces the encrypted access-control database file. "MAKEDB" is a security database compiler. As personnel come and go, join one project and leave another, the text file is edited, user names are added or deleted, users are assigned to or removed from groups and then the input text file is recompiled. No alteration of any archive file or AccessList is needed.

Protecting Archive Files

Usually, a archive file is stored write-protected to prevent accidental erasure. It is important to note that archive files should be backed up with the system just like any other file. Nothing can prevent a knowledgeable user from deleting archive files or any other type file if they are bent on doing so.

Summary

Security of the system is very important. The PVCS tool set provides a mechanism by which groups and users may be assigned specific rights and restrictions. Members of a group do not need to have the same rights and restrictions. PVCS provides password protection for environments that do not normally have such protection. The PVCS access-control database is encrypted and contains user, group, and privilege definitions.

Questions

1. Give an example of why an entry level programmer may need more restrictions than a senior level programmer based solely on the experience levels of each.

2. Create four group definitions for a single group that will permit differing access rights and restrictions depending upon the type of file accessed.

3. Using your group definitions establish the AccessList for four file types so that only certain operations upon that file type may be performed by the group.

6

The Archive File

The Archive File Components

An *archive file* is a version control file under the control of PVCS. Users do not edit archive files. PVCS edits archive files. The user extracts a copy of a revision to edit from an archive file. He or she works on the copy of the file stored in the archive file, not on the archive file. The archive file itself contains vital information about the change history of the source file that the archive file is tracking.

Refer to Fig. 6.1. An archive file contains a listing of attributes that describe its characteristics and properties, a description of the file it contains, the latest revision of that file, a complete revision history, and one or more compact forms of data used to rebuild previous revisions. These compact forms of data are called *deltas*. Note that the contents of the archive file may not be in the order listed above. Their order is not important, their presence is.

Attributes

Each archive file inherits attributes when it is created. The nature of these inherited attributes depends upon the current settings of configuration attribute parameters. These parameters are set at program invocation when configuration files are processed. If an attribute parameter is set in the Master Configuration File, a user may be able to override and alter the setting in a local configuration file. The last setting of an attribute parameter is the one that takes effect. Attribute resetting can be prevented by using the configuration parameter Disallow in the Master Configuration File. Refer to Chap. 10, Setting Up and Configuring PVCS, for more information about configurations.

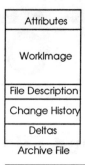

Figure 6.1   Archive file contents.

All archive file attributes are initially set when an archive file is first created. A subset of the configuration parameters defines such things as how the archive file is stored, what kind of access is permitted, and who has the access. A list of archive file attributes is displayed in Table 6.1.

TABLE 6.1   Archive File Attributes

Attribute	Definition
AccessList	Users and Groups who have access rights to the logfile
WorkFileName	The name of the file to produce when requested
CommentPrefix	Used for embedded comments
NewLine	Also used for embedded comments
Compression	What parts, if any, of the logfile are compressed
Exclusivelock	Can only one person have one lock?
ExpandKeyWords	If keywords are present, should they be expanded
Owner	Who or what is the owner of the file.
Translate	Translate between VMS or UNIX and DOS or OS/2
WriteProtect	Is the logfile stored write-protected?

AccessList

The "AccessList" archive file attribute parameter specifies those users or groups of users who have access rights to the archive file. PVCS always uses the AccessList archive file attribute parameter to determine accessibility. This is true even if enhanced access control, (discussed later), is employed. As discussed in the previous chapter, the AccessList configuration parameter from which the archive file inherits its AccessList archive file attribute should indicate those groups having access to the archive file, rather than the names of individuals.

CheckLock

The "CheckLock" attribute parameter tells PVCS to ensure that the person checking in a new revision is the same person who owns the lock. The archive file attribute parameter may be set to "NoCheck-Lock", in which case PVCS is only interested in the presence of a lock rather than who owns the lock. The default setting of the CheckLock attribute parameter is CheckLock. The NoCheckLock setting would only be appropriate in a one or two person shop with good interpersonal communications. It is recommended that the default value, CheckLock, be used and that the CheckLock attribute parameter be disallowed in the Master Configuration File with the Disallow configuration parameter. For readability, you may wish to disallow NoCheckLock in the Master Configuration File. Disallowing NoCheckLock has the exact same effect as disallowing Check-Lock. Disallowing a privilege produces the exact same effect as disallowing a restriction. Once one is disallowed, the other is automatically disallowed as well.

CommentPrefix

The "CommentPrefix" archive file attribute is used only if the keyword Log is used in the file. Keywords are discussed later in this chapter. The Log keyword causes the author's change description to be automatically added to the file's header each time that a new revision is checked in. When setting up CommentPrefix in a configuration file, multiple settings are allowed that reference a comment line prefix to a specific file type where the type of file is determined by its suffix. If an archive file is created for a work file whose file suffix is listed in the configuration file declarations, it will inherit the correct comment prefix. PVCS provides many default values for CommentPrefix for various file types.

Compression

The "Compress" archive file attribute determines if archive file compression will be used, and if so, what parts of the archive file are compressed. The Compress configuration parameter provides a mechanism by which different file types may receive different degrees of compression. There are three degrees of compression, full compression, delta compression, and work image compression. Full compression is a combination of delta compression, and work image compression. Delta compression compresses only the change records and is implemented by using the "CompressDelta" configuration parameter. Work image compression, obtained by using the "Compress-WorkImage" configuration parameter, compresses only the latest revision, which is stored full and complete. Compression saves storage space for a small performance price. The compression algorithm is very efficient and very fast.

ExclusiveLock

The "ExclusiveLock" archive file attribute parameter permits only one locked revision in the entire archive file. This prohibits one person from editing a branch or early revision while another person edits yet another revision. An example of this might be the latest revision. The default setting is "NoExclusiveLock", which permits multiple locks in an archive file. Regardless of the setting of this parameter, one person may own only one lock of one revision at any given time unless the "MultiLock" configuration parameter is in effect. The MultiLock configuration parameter allows a user to own multiple locks in an archive file and to allow multiple users to lock the same revision of an archive file.

ExpandKeywords

The "ExpandKeywords" archive file attribute parameter instructs PVCS to expand keywords upon check-in. Expanding keywords allows PVCS to automatically update and add information to a new revision. The use of keywords is highly recommended, but requires some care for certain types of files. Some word processors do not store data sequentially in files. The number of bytes in a section is stored and sections saved, not necessarily in consecutive order. Changing the byte count of a section by expanding the keywords will cause these programs to fail. There is, however, a way to prevent the increase in byte count normally caused by expanding keywords. To do so, use a double colon immediately after the literal keyword, followed by the number of characters you desire in the expansion represented by the character 'x' immediately after the colon. (For example, $Revision::xxxx$.)

NewLine

The "NewLine" archive file attribute parameter is the logical match for the CommentPrefix archive file attribute parameter. NewLine tells PVCS how to terminate a comment line inserted as a result of expanding the Log keyword. Like CommentPrefix, file types may be specified to differentiate the line termination from one file type to another.

Owner

The "Owner" archive file attribute parameter specifies the owner of the archive file. To simplify report generation for a specific project, it is recommended that the Owner parameter be set to the project name. By using arguments to PVCS report generating commands, it is easy to specify files by the author or owner. If the owner is a project name, then it becomes easy to specify a project name to determine the status of project files.

Translate

The "Translate" archive file attribute parameter is used when the file server is running the VMS or UNIX operating systems. Under VMS, PVCS is instructed to translate end-of-line characters to carriage return plus line feed. Under UNIX, Translate causes PVCS to convert the end-of-line sequence from line feed to carriage return plus line feed.

WriteProtect

The "WriteProtect" archive file attribute parameter specifies that the archive file be stored in write protected mode. This default can be altered to "NoWriteProtect" which will, of course, not store the archive files in write protected mode. Naturally, it is recommended that the default value, WriteProtect be left in force.

Work Image

The latest revision on the trunk of the archive file revision tree is the work image. The work image is the latest revision in whole and complete form. The reason it is stored whole and complete is for performance. Because it is whole and complete, no computation is required to construct the latest revision before producing the working copy. Since most requests for a working copy will be for the latest revision, most requests can be honored with little or no delay.

Another reason to have the latest revision whole and complete is that storing it in that fashion greatly simplifies the process of adding a new revision to an archive file. Instead of having to compute the latest stored revision to compare it to the new incoming revision, the comparison can be made immediately. This feature becomes very important as the number of revisions grows.

File Description

When an archive file is first created, it contains no revisions. The archive file has a name and attributes only. PVCS will ask the archive file creator for a description of the workfile. The description given should be one that describes the workfile, its purpose, its class, the project to which it belongs, or any other verbiage that will be useful to someone who needs to know what the file is, not just what is in it.

File Revision History

When the first revision is checked in, PVCS comments it automatically as the "Initial Revision". Once a second revision is checked in, the archive file begins to maintain a file revision history. For each revision, the date stamp of the edited workfile when it was checked in is maintained. PVCS stores the date stamp of when the file was checked in. Three numbers representing lines added, deleted or moved are maintained as is the name of the author of the new revision and any comments the author makes about the change.

Change Descriptions

When a user checks in a new revision, PVCS asks the user for a description of the change. The supplied description becomes a permanent part of the archive's file revision history. The description should indicate the nature of changes made and why they were made. If the entered description merely says "fixed bugs", then the next user or anyone examining the file will not have a very good indication of what really happened to the file. It is important to include a complete description.

The default editor provided by the PVCS command line interface is not adequate for lengthy descriptions. Once a line has been entered, it cannot be edited. To repair the comment, the command must be aborted and the process restarted. For this reason, PVCS provides a mechanism by which any editor program may be invoked automatically by PVCS. An editor gives the user the ability to correct spelling mistakes or grammatical errors or even repair the content of the description without aborting the command. To set PVCS up to call an editor automatically, a parameter, "VCSEdit", is added to a PVCS configuration file that indicates the invocation of the editor. Usually, this parameter is added to the user's local configuration file rather than to the Master Configuration File, which dictates actions for all users.

Yet another mechanism provided by PVCS is the ability to read the comments automatically from an existing file. The user can create the file using his or her favorite text editor, save it, and then reference it from the PVCS command line. This method simplifies the maintenance of local configuration files. The command line in this case is illustrated in Fig. 6.2.

A third mechanism provided by PVCS is the automatic inclusion of comment files of a given file suffix. This method uses the configuration parameter "MessageSuffix" in a configuration file. MessageSuffix is used to construct a file name suffix from the name of the workfile or archive file. It is a logical map, that is, it uses fixed and variable characters to alter the file suffix. The default MessageSuffix is "??@___". This six character map tells PVCS that the first two characters of the original file suffix are to be used as is and the third character will always be "@". The final three positions of the character map tell PVCS what character to use if one of the variable characters is not present. Refer to Fig. 6.3 to view some file name examples.

To use the MessageSuffix as defined above, the configuration parameter MessageSuffix does not have to be defined in any PVCS configuration file. However, if for some reason the default character map is not appropriate, it may be redefined in a PVCS configuration file. Figure 6.4 illustrates file name computation when MessageSuffix has been redefined by to "??TCMT".

To mandate the use of MessageSuffix, it can be included in the Master Configuration File. This method also simplifies the command line interface as the user does not need to specify the name of the file that contains his or her comments. The user command line in this case is illustrated in Fig. 6.5.

Deltas

Deltas are change records. There is a delta record for each revision in an archive file except the very last revision that was checked into the

```
PUT -m@<comment_file_name> <workfile_name>

                          or

PUT -m@<comment_file_name> <archive_file_name>
```

Figure 6.2   Command line to include comments from a comment file.

Default MESSAGESUFFIX	"??@___"

Original File Name	Comment File Name
TEST.COB	TEST.CO@
TEST.C	TEST.C_@
TEST	TEST._@
TEST.FOR	TEST.FO@

Figure 6.3   Use of MESSAGESUFFIX configuration parameter.

trunk of the archive file. In each delta record is the difference between two revisions, stored in a very compact manner, that permits reconstruction of one revision from the other. In addition, the author, date of check-in, date of revision and author's comments are stored in the delta record.

The Trunk

The trunk is the name given to the main development path of the module. The trunk begins at the very first revision checked in and ends with the very latest revision checked in that is not a member of a branch. The archive file revisions form a structure that resembles a tree. Refer to Fig. 6.6.

Branches

Branches represent alternate development paths for a module. A branch may represent a port of the module, such as the same application on a different platform. A branch may represent a customized application, like an application program with a customized copyright display and customized functionality sold to a value-added reseller. A branch might also represent an emergency fix.

User defined MESSAGESUFFIX	"??TCMT"

Original File Name	Comment File Name
TEST.COB	TEST.COT
TEST.C	TEST.CMT
TEST	TEST.CMT
TEST.FOR	TEST.FOT

Figure 6.4   Use of user-defined message suffix configuration parameter.

```
PUT -m@ <workfile_name>
```

or

```
PUT -m@ <archive_file_name>
```

**Figure 6.5   Command line to include comments
from MESSAGESUFFIX file.**

The case of the emergency fix is especially useful. Imagine that a major release has been made within the last few months and that today a customer calls the support line with a fatal problem. A serious bug is found! When the programming team goes to fix the bug, it is found that the module has already been modified in preparation for the next release. You cannot fix the bug with the latest revision because it will introduce undocumented and untested functionality. The solution is to produce a branch off of the released revision, fix the bug in the branch revision, move the release version label over to the fixed revision on the branch, and rerelease the product. Now, the bug may or may not still live in the modified revision that is the latest on the trunk. To ensure that the bug fix is implemented in the trunk revisions, simply merge the repair branch with the main development path and the bug fix is incorporated into the modified revision. Of course it will need to be tested and verified, but any change made to source code has that requirement.

The Tip Revision

The tip revision of the trunk or branch is the latest revision checked into the trunk or branch. The tip always represents the latest incarna-

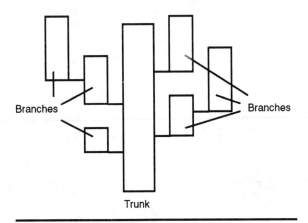

Figure 6.6   Archive file's tree-shaped structure.

tion of its respective arm of the archive file revision tree. The tip of a branch is the latest checked into that branch, the tip of the trunk is the latest checked into the trunk.

Revision Numbering

Revision numbering is automatic. The automatic numbering can be overridden if desired. Refer to Fig. 6.7. Usually the first revision stored in the archive file is assigned the revision number 1.0. The first digit is the revision major number, the second is its minor number. The second revision checked in would be 1.1, followed by 1.2, and so on. It may be that a decision is made to number the first revision 0.0 instead of 1.0, thereby reserving 1.0 for the development baseline after the first major release. Starting with revision 0.0 is a common practice.

Branches are numbered in a manner by which the revision from which they emanate is readily identifiable. The revision number of a branch revision has four or more components depending upon whether it emanates from the trunk or from another branch. Refer to Fig. 6.8. Note that the branch that emanates from revision 1.3, starting with revision 1.3.1.0, has 1.3.1 as its default major number. The branch that emanates from branch revision 1.3.1.2 has a major number of 1.3.1.2.1.

Embedded Information Keywords

As mentioned earlier, most revision control products, including PVCS, provide a mechanism by which revision information can be embedded into source documents automatically. The method for accomplishing this makes use of what are called *keywords*. Keywords are identified by the revision control program and expanded by the program into meaningful text. Under PVCS, you have the option of turning keyword

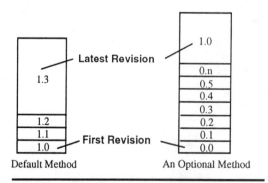

Figure 6.7   Archive file revision numbering.

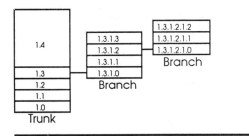

Figure 6.8   Archive file default revision numbering scheme.

expansion off or on and defining the form and content for some of the keywords. Keywords expand to different values for different revisions and reflect the contents of the current workfile, regardless of from where in the archive file tree the workfile was extracted.

$Workfile$

The $Workfile$ keyword represents the name of the source file that is extracted from PVCS when a user retrieves a copy of a revision. The workfile and archive file have different names. They are related in base name only, the suffix is altered by the configuration parameter "ArchiveSuffix". Each archive file stores as one of its attributes, the name of the workfile it is to produce. If you alter the name of the archive file, it will still produce a workfile of the same name as before. To alter the workfile name, the VCS administrative command must be used.

The $Workfile$ keyword expands to the name of the workfile.

$Archive$

The $Archive$ keyword expands to be the name of the archive file from which the workfile was extracted. Usually, the workfile and the archive file have similar names differing only in the file suffix. This may not always be the case. For example, the archive file for the module "foo.c" is normally named "foo.c_v". If the archive file is renamed to "fred.c_v" it will still produce the workfile "foo.c". The two names, "fred.c_v" and "foo.c" are not in any way related. In this case, the $Archive$ keyword is especially needed.

$Revision$

The $Revision$ keyword expands to the current revision number of the workfile. This keyword is especially helpful in that you know what revision you are working on. This information can be crucial if multiple edits on revisions from the archive file are occurring. Knowing the originating revision number can be a great help in determining which revision of an archive file to lock if an edit has been performed without owning a lock. Naturally, there is some danger in this in that the revision may have been previously superseded. However, the danger is not real because the new revision will be checked in as a branch.

$Author$

The $Author$ keyword expands to the name of the author of a revision. Whoever checked the revision in is the author of that revision.

$Date$

The $Date$ keyword expands to the date and time that the revision was checked in. Sometimes it is necessary to check dates of revisions to determine when an event happened. This is especially true when the event had a negative impact upon the system.

$Modtime$

The $Modtime$ keyword expands to the date and time that was current for the workfile when it was checked in. In other words, the date stamp of the file is used for the file modification time. This action may be altered in a configuration file by specifying "ExpandKeywords Touch", in which case the file modification time is identical to the file check-in time. The "Touch" parameter tells PVCS to give the current date stamp (the time of check-in) to the file modification time.

$Header$

The $Header$ keyword is a combination of the $Archive$, $Revision$, $Date$ and $Author$ keywords. When $Header$ expands it specifies the archive file name, revision number, check-in date, and author of the revision.

Log

The Log keyword expands to include the change description entered by the author at check-in time. Log will insert a comment line whose prefix is determined by the configuration parameter CommentPrefix and whose suffix is determined by the configuration parameter New-Line. An example is shown in Fig. 6.9. In the first case, the default CommentPrefix and NewLine are used for a comment in a C programming language source file. The "\n" character specifies a new line. In

Default	
COMMENTPREFIX.C " * " NEWLINE.C "\n"	* My comments are * my business
Altered	
COMMENTPREFIX.C "/* " NEWLINE.C "*/\n	/* My comments are */ /* my business */

Figure 6.9   Effect of configuration parameters on Log expansion.

the second case, both CommentPrefix and NewLine have been altered to cause a complete comment structure to be inserted. As can be readily seen, the CommentPrefix and NewLine parameters are for convenience and customization of Log comment expansion.

It is highly recommended that each and every source file contain a header in which several keywords are used. At the very least, $Workfile$, $Revision$ and $Date$. An example of a C programming language header is illustrated in Fig. 6.10.

Change Descriptions

When a user checks in a new revision, he or she is asked to enter a change description. It is this change description that is embedded into the source document by the Log keyword. However, it is also stored as part of the file revision history. The author's comments are preserved whether or not the Log keyword is used.

Revision Storage Methods

Recall that there are two methods for storing revisions. Forward deltas that use the original revision as a base and store deltas from that

```
/*
 *      $Workfile$ $Revision$
 *      Checked in $Date$ by $Author$
 *      File description (can be identical to initial checkin description)
 *      $Log$
 *
 */
```

Figure 6.10   Sample source document header C programming language.

revision on, and *reverse deltas* that use the latest revision as the base and store deltas for prior revisions. The reverse delta is the fastest because it stores the latest revision whole and complete and therefore requires little or no computation to retrieve the latest revision. Forward delta storage stores the original revision whole and complete, therefore, as more revisions are added, computation time increases linearly.

PVCS stores trunk revisions in reverse delta format for speed and stores branches in forward delta format because there is no other way. When computing a branch revision, PVCS starts with the latest revision from the trunk, moves backwards until it reaches the revision from which the branch emanates, then moves forward up the branch.

Summary

The archive file maintains all pertinent information regarding the workfile and all its revisions. Keywords can be used to imbed some of this information into the source file. PVCS uses reverse delta storage to minimize computation and maximize performance. The archive file has a trunk and may have branches. The revisions stored in an archive file form a revision tree.

Questions

1. Explain in detail why branches cannot be stored in reverse delta format.

2. Why have a multiple-file database to store the revision information? Why not use a single-file database? What advantages are there to the multiple-file format? What disadvantages?

7

Fundamentals of Revision Management

The Manager's Perspective

The perspective of revision management from the manager's role depends upon the responsibilities of the individual manager. Typically, the manager is not concerned with the number of revisions it took to get a project to a given state, milestone or release. What is important is the production and quality of the revisions that make up the project at any given time. First-line managers are more likely to care about the growth and development of revisions as they relate to the production of a working body of source documents. The higher the manager's level, the less concern with individual revisions and the more concern with versions and, possibly, promotion groups. Of course, there are always exceptions to the rule.

Generally, however, managers are not concerned with revisions that are transitory or incomplete. For example, if ten revisions of a module are traversed on the path to a bug fix, the manager would be concerned with the first and last revisions only—the broken revision and the fixed revision. In this regard, many development organizations maintain two sets of revision database files. One set is for the programming team, the other is for release or milestone revisions. Using two sets of revision control database systems provides the programmer with the ability to experiment and perhaps find the elegant and efficient algorithm while providing management with a concise and definitive release revision sequence. While this appears to be similar to the dual maintenance problem at first glance, it is not. There are not multiple copies of a common module floating about the system. The second database is used to reflect the state of the first database at critical times, such as a release or milestone. The first database contains many revisions, the second contains a subset thereof.

Another aspect of revision management perspective is the determination of what types of documents are stored under revision control. At a minimum, and rightfully so, management will expect that source code modules be maintained under revision control. Typically, the concern for revision management is only for source code modules. As configuration management techniques become more widely used and accepted, revision management will also find inroads into disciplines that either have not used revision management at all or have used it minimally.

Documentation, Requirements, and Specifications

To date, not many organizations require or even use revision management for the control of documentation. If revision control is used at all, it is usually only to set off changes in a new revision from changes in the last revision for review purposes. The changes are usually highlighted with some kind of mark, sometimes called change bars, or the altered paragraphs are enclosed in boxes to set them apart.

One class of document that is subject to change and is largely overlooked is the specification or requirement document. Often, a specification will change with little or no notification as to when the change occurred and what the change consisted of. Sometimes the right people are informed, sometimes they find out by accident. Very often, the programmer who implements the requirements and specifications is not informed until significant work has already been accomplished against the old specification or requirements document. Sometimes, the change in the specification comes as a very nasty surprise to the programmer. A surprise that discards long hours of programming as time wasted and promises many more long hours of programming new modules and editing old to meet the new specification. This problem is a lot more pervasive than is generally acknowledged. In fact, there are very few organizations in which the maintenance and distribution of specifications is what it should be.

All of the above-mentioned causes for severe headache and stress can be eliminated if the specifications, requirements, and documentation are kept under revision control. Not only are cures to the ailments found, vast improvements in program accuracy and programmer productivity are realized. The ability to perform change and release tracking of specifications is an additional benefit derived from using revision management techniques for all files or documents that are subject to change over any period of time.

The Audit Trail

One very useful collection of information that can be generated by incorporating revision management techniques is the audit trail. An audit trail provides a method for tracking footprints in the development path of any given project. It does not matter if the project is software, hardware, or documentation.

The audit trail is a file that contains a listing of events that caused an alteration of either the state or the contents of an archive file. If a revision is checked out for edit, the archive file's state changes. If a revision is checked in, the archive file's state changes. If the system administrator changes a permission or attribute in an archive file, its state has been altered. All such actions result in an entry in the audit trail that tell the reader of the file performed the deed, when they did it, what file they did it to and exactly what it is that they did.

The audit trail is especially helpful in managing revisions in that it becomes easy to obtain information about the project as a whole. How many files does Fred have checked out for edit? How many files have been altered by Sue? How long has Jack had "average.cob" checked out? What is happening with a given file? Who is doing what?

The Author's Perspective

From the author's perspective, implementing revision management is wonderful. If a programming goal is reached, for example, a programmer finally gets some particularly nasty function to operate properly after a long drawn-out algorithmic battle, the working revision can be checked in and maintained for posterity and in case of emergency. The feeling of security in maintaining one's accomplishments is a good feeling.

Another benefit, and one of great consequence to programmer efficiency, is that of protected experimentation. If a body of code needs to be made more efficient for performance reasons, or it needs to be improved for any other reason, the programmer can safely experiment with the code without fear of prolonged edits to recover a previous state should the experiment fail.

Use the example of the performance requirement to show how revision management can benefit the programmer in this context. When the programmer evaluates the body of code that operates too slowly, he or she may come up with several ideas to improve the performance. Which one is the best? The answer to that question is unknown without verified evidence. Without revision management, when an experiment fails, the programmer usually reedits the file removing the experiment and perhaps trying another method. Much time is spent in reediting that could better be used in performing the experiments. Using revision management, if an experiment does not work, the programmer need not reedit, but simply obtain a fresh copy without the experimental changes from the revision management system. Instead of editing code only to have to change it back, the programmer simply deletes the experiment and recovers.

If several experiments must be compared, the programmer can create a branch revision to store the code for each experiment. When all is said and done and one experiment proves the best solution to the problem, the alternate branch revisions can be deleted. The selected revision can then be checked in as the next revision on the trunk (or branch) from which the original revision was checked out and the branch revision (from the trunk or development branch) can be deleted.

The ability to restore revisions to a given condition without reediting them to accomplish the task is of great benefit and saves countless hours of programming time.

Another benefit to the author is that configuration management provides debugging tools. If, for example, a system works fairly well on one day, but several days later it crashes, the author can simply determine the modules that have changed since the system worked. Once the altered modules are determined, the exact changes to any likely culprits can be examined to determine the exact cause of the error. Naturally, all changes can be examined if necessary. Once the error is found, it can be repaired. The ability to isolate and identify the changes made is a great time-saving advantage.

If the error still cannot be determined, then the changes made to one module affected some other module. Using the where used document report, the author can easily determine all modules affected by the changes and more readily and speedily find and repair the problem.

Issues of Granularity

As can be seen, the perspective of revision management is determined largely by position in the development team. While management could care less about the intermediate revision that contains an algorithmic error, the programmer may have accomplished some goal aside from the obvious error that deserves revision storage. Therefore, it should not be up to higher-level management to dictate the qualifications for revision storage. The user can usually determine the revisions that are worthy of storage in one context or another.

The project

As far as the project is concerned, only those revisions that have direct impact upon the development process of the project need to be maintained under revision management. However, it is sometimes difficult to differentiate between revisions of intermediate or transitory value and those that are of consequence. In general, any revision that completes some programming goal is worthy of storage.

The author

From a programmer's point of view, any revision that constitutes several hours work or editing deserves storage regardless of syntactical error or comment deficiencies. If work has been expended, it is worth storing. Once stored, the revision can be edited to incorporate comments or to fix syntactical errors, and a new revision stored containing the additions and repairs.

The author's secret stash

As mentioned above, some organizations will maintain two sets of revisions, one for milestones and releases and the other for work in progress. Many organizations do not do so. Regardless of whether the organization divides the archive file database, it is sometimes of benefit for yet another revision set to be stored, the programmer's personal revision control database. The organization's revision control database(s) are stored on the file server. The programmer's database is stored on his or her own workstation. The addition of a personal revision database provides the programmer with the ability to maintain his or her work regardless of the network's status. If the network goes down, the programmer can still accomplish work and maintain a development history. Not only does this personal revision stash provide revision security in the event of a network failure, it also provides a mechanism by which only revisions of consequence need be stored on the network. Those revisions with deficiencies can be stored in the programmer's own secret stash and perhaps never uploaded to the server. Revisions are uploaded to the network when the work in progress represented by the revision has been completed to the satisfaction of the programmer.

Archiving an Archive File

There are two ways to create archive files under PVCS. The first is by using the administrative command "VCS -i" to initialize an archive file that contains attributes and a workfile description, but contains no first revision. The second method depends upon the configuration parameter, AutoCreate, which specifies that an archive file is to be created whenever a file is checked in and no archive file already exists for that file. In this case, the archive file is initialized with attributes, a workfile description, and a first revision. There are some specific dangers associated with using the AutoCreate method.

When PVCS attempts to work on an archive file, it searches a path of directories specified by the configuration parameter VCSDir to find the appropriate archive file. While the VCSDir parameter can be tightly controlled by incorporating a conditional construct in the Master Configuration File, it is usually found in the user's local configuration file. The reason for using the VCSDir configuration parameter in a local configuration file is that a programmer will typically work on more that one file or set of files at a time. A programmer may set up several working directories, each of which is associated with a set of archive files by having a local configuration file in the working directory that points to a different archive file directory. By changing working directories, the programmer automatically changes the archive file directory from which he or she works.

The danger in using AutoCreate is especially severe under the above conditions. The first and the most deadly danger is the fact that if the user's VCSDir setting has changed, (perhaps by changing working directories), then PVCS may not be able to find the archive file for a given workfile. For example, a programmer working on two related program files copies a workfile from its working directory to the working directory of the other related file. The programmer works on the file and then checks it in. The problem is that the programmer is not working in the correct working directory. PVCS cannot find the archive file and, because AutoCreate is in effect, creates a new archive file. Now, multiple archive files exist for the same workfile. If the programmer was not paying close attention when the check-in occurred, the programmer may be unaware that a new single revision archive file exists. The next time the programmer changes to the proper working directory and checks out a copy of the workfile from the original archive file, his or her changes will appear to have been lost to that great bit-bucket in the sky. Anger, frustration, and other negative emotions may color the air around said programmer for quite some time unless he or she considers the course of events that he or she performed and realize that he or she has created a second archive file. The programmer then must find the second archive file, extract the revision, and then check that revision into the original archive file. After the programmer has recovered the modified module and checked it into the real archive file, he or she may delete the newly created archive file.

Another problem with using AutoCreate is that new archive files may be created without plan. These may range from an inadvertent duplication to a deviation from design. In some instances, it may be a personal project that has nothing to do with the organization's plans or products. While these consequences may not harm the single programmer or small development team organization, they can be disastrous for a networked development environment. For these reasons, it is recommended that the AutoCreate parameter be disallowed and all archive files be created specifically with the administrative "VCS -i" command.

Using the Archive File Revision Tree

We have discussed the fact that an archive file has a trunk and that the trunk can have branches. We have mentioned the fact that branches can have branches. The trunk represents the main development path. Branches provide the ability to manage alternate development. The emergency bug-fix use for a branch has been mentioned. There are other uses for branches.

The trunk

The trunk of the archive file is used to maintain revisions that make up the primary development path of a project. The trunk is where algorithmic and programmatic development occurs. The trunk is where the functionality of a module is developed and defined. If a project is to reside and run on only one platform and will have no custom modifications or alterations, the trunk is the only consequential part of the archive file revision tree.

Archive file branches

Branches can be used for the emergency bug-fix scenario as discussed previously. Refer to Fig. 7.1, in which revision 1.4 represents the flawed release of a product. Revision 1.4, which represents the release version

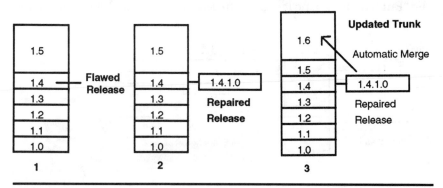

Figure 7.1 The emergency bug-fix scenario.

of the product, has already been superseded by the development team. Revision 1.4.1.0 represents the repaired release revision and becomes the new member of the revised released product. Revision 1.6 on the trunk contains the bug fix and all modifications made to revision 1.4 that were contained in revision 1.5. The bug fix is stored in the branch revision, and is folded back into the trunk immediately to ensure that the fix is incorporated into the main development path and to ensure that the next release of the product will not reintroduce the bug. The fix is folded in with an automatic merge facility.

Other than the emergency bug fix, branches represent an alternate development path for projects. Branches are especially useful in maintaining custom modifications or alternate platform development paths. In Fig. 7.2, the trunk was used to develop a DOS application. Once the DOS application was completed, the application was ported to Microsoft Windows, OS/2, OS/2 Presentation Manager, and UNIX. In addition, a custom DOS product was developed for a large company, XYZ Inc., to relabel as their own for sales and distribution to their clients and customers.

While DOS, OS/2, Windows, Presentation Manager, and UNIX were used in the above example, the same paradigm is applicable to the mainframe development environment. Each branch can be used to represent a different mainframe platform or dialect of the COBOL language.

How to Create Revisions

Once an archive file has been created, it contains zero or one revision, depending upon whether or not the AutoCreate configuration parameter was enabled and the user took advantage of it. Refer to Chapter 10 for more information about AutoCreate. The use of AutoCreate is not recommended. Assume that the newly created archive file has no revisions. In this case, the first time that a revision is checked in, using the "Put" command, no locking is necessary. Because there is no change

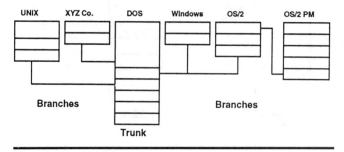

Figure 7.2 Archive file branch alternate development paths.

to describe, the first revision will automatically receive the change description, "Initial Revision". From here on out, revisions must be locked by an authorized developer before a new revision can be checked in.

Revision locking

There are several ways to lock a revision. The first and most commonly used is to lock the revision when a copy of the workfile is extracted by using "Get -l". The "-l" or locking option specifies that the file is being checked out for edit. Note that at any time, any revision can be checked out for browsing purposes. The browse copy of the workfile is usually write-protected unless checked out with the "-w" or write enable option.

Sometimes a programmer will check out a write enabled browse copy only to discover that some editing is required. The normal procedure is to check out the file again using the "-l" option. Sometimes, in the heat of the moment, the second check-out is forgotten and editing commences. When this happens and the author goes to check in the new revision, he or she is told that they own no lock in the archive file. In this case, the programmer can check to see which revision he or she has, (hopefully, the $Revision$ keyword is in use) and apply a lock to that revision using the administrative command with the locking option, "VCS -l." It is very important that the correct revision be locked. Suppose that while the author is editing the file, another author locks the revision, completes an edit, and checks in a new revision. If the first author now locks the new revision and checks in his or her work, he or she may lose the second author's changes. The changes are not lost, but the loss will need to be discovered and the lost changes recovered. If for no other reason than this, the $Revision$ keyword should be used in each and every file header.

The third method is used when continuing work on the module will occur. In this case, the author can check in the new revision with the "Put -l" command, which specifies to check in the new revision and immediately lock it with the author's identification and preserve the workfile for the author's use.

Checking in the new revision

Once editing has been accomplished on a workfile, it needs to be checked in and a new revision created. The command to accomplish this task is the "Put" command. "Put" first verifies that the author has permission to check in a new revision, then "Put" verifies that the author who is attempting to check in the new revision owns the lock on the previous revision. If these conditions are met, the "Put" command checks in a new revision.

Commenting the change

The "Put" command requests a change description for the new revision. As discussed previously, there are several ways in which the change description can be entered. The change description entered should not be a generic statement, such as, "Fixed a bug". Instead, the change description should be specific, something like "Fixed a divide overflow problem in the consolidation section." The comment should be such that any other person who views the file can determine exactly what was accomplished. The change description should be augmented with in-line comments in the case of the modified module containing source code.

Revision unlocking

When a new revision is checked in using the "Put" command, the locked revision is automatically unlocked. However, sometimes a revision is checked out for edit, which locks the revision, and no changes are made. In this case, there are several methods to remove the lock.

The first and most straightforward is the use of the administrative command, "VCS -u" which allows an author to remove his or her lock without checking in a new revision. The "-u" option to the "VCS" command simply specifies that the lock owned by the person who invoked the command be removed from the archive file regardless of which revision the person locked.

The "VCS -u" command can be used to specify an exact revision to unlock by identifying that revision in the command line. The command "VCS -u1.1" will unlock revision 1.1 only if one of two conditions is met. Either the person who invoked the command owns the lock and has "UnLock" privileges or the person has "BreakLock" privileges and thus can break or remove any other authors locks.

How to Destroy Revisions

Sometimes an author will check in a revision only to discover that an error has been made, the revision should not have been checked in. In this case, if the author has the correct permission level, "DeleteRev" or "DeleteRevTip", he or she can issue a "VDEL *archive_filename*" command and the revision will be deleted. This use of the "VDEL" command deletes the revision that has just been checked in. However, if another author has locked the revision since it was checked in, the "VDEL" command will not work and the person attempting to delete the revision will be notified that the revision is locked and cannot be deleted. If the tip revision is deleted, it is as if it was never checked in. It is completely lost.

Sometimes, a decision can be made to "clean up" the revision tree by removing unused or unwanted revisions. The "VDEL" command can be used to delete a range of revisions as well as individual revisions.

PVCS will always ask for specific permission to delete a revision or range thereof regardless of the user having the permission to do so in the first place. Naturally, the user without such permission will not get so far as to have PVCS ask if they are really sure that they want to delete the revisions. Deleting revisions is not trivial in consequence and requires great care. The person deleting revisions should know exactly what they intend to do before they start.

That which cannot be destroyed

The changes made in any deleted revision are not lost, but instead are combined with the first nondeleted revision to insure that all previous revisions can be reconstructed. No revision that is locked or that is the root of a branch may be deleted.

That which is destroyed

When a revision is deleted, it may never again be reconstructed. The change record including author name, modification date and check-in date are lost. Change comments for deleted revisions are lost unless the Log keyword has embedded them into the source document.

How to create branches

There are two ways to create branches. The first method is automatic and happens when an earlier revision (not the tip) is checked out for edit. PVCS notifies the user that locking the revision will create a branch at check-out time and ask for permission to continue. When the edited workfile from an early revision is checked in, the branch will be started automatically. This, of course, assumes that the author has StartBranch privileges.

The second method is used when a branch off of the tip revision is required. When the revised workfile is checked in, if the author uses "Put -fb", a branch revision will be created rather than a new revision on the development path. The "-fb" option, or "force branch" tells PVCS not to expand upon the development path, but rather to create an alternate development path off of the tip revision of the current development path. The development path may itself be an alternate development path, thus the "-fb" option would create a branch off of a branch.

Summary

An archive file may contain many development paths for a project. Alternate paths may represent varying hardware or software platform ports and are stored in archive file branches. For each module, there may be one or more archive files depending upon the development environment. Regardless of the number of archive files for each module, only one is the master archive file. Secondary archive files may be used to represent an individual's efforts or be used to track specific milestones or release levels.

Archive files are created using the administrative "VCS" command or by use of the AutoCreate configuration parameter. Use of the AutoCreate configuration parameter is not recommended in network environments. A new revision can only be checked in if the previous revision has been locked by the author attempting to check in the new revision. Caution should be exercised when deleting archive file revisions.

Questions

1. How could you ensure that no duplicate and incomplete archive files are created if the AutoCreate configuration parameter is used? Under what circumstances would AutoCreate be an appropriate setting? Why?

2. When deleting a range of revisions, only those revisions that are not locked or the root of a branch are automatically preserved. Revisions that contain version labels that identify them as part of a release or milestone can be inadvertently deleted. What procedure could be used to prevent the inadvertent deletion of version specific revisions? What general policy could be developed to prevent this occurrence? Can it be accomplished solely by permission levels? Why or why not?

8

Fundamentals of Version Control

One key facility in the software development arena is the ability to track the components of a project in terms of versions of the product. When this is accomplished, it becomes a simple matter to reconstruct any or all of the project as it stood on a given date.

What Is a Version?

A version is an instance of a system, a collection of software programs or other types of files that when combined produce an instance of a system that performs a specific function. For example, a complete version might be a collection of source code file revisions that, when compiled and linked, produce the beta version of a function that produces amortization data. Another example would be a collection of document files that when combined produce release level 2 of a user manual. Yet another example would be a collection of include and source files that when combined in some manner produce the current working version of an executable program.

A version of a system may represent a given milestone in the development life cycle, a specific or custom release of a product or program, or perhaps a collection of working revisions targeted for the next release of a product. Basically, a version of a system can represent anything you desire.

Static and Dynamic Versions

Most versions of a system are static, that is, unchanging. For example, when a software product is ready for beta test, the revision levels of all modules associated with the system at the time of the beta test release will not change. If revision 1.13 of module "average.cob" is included in the beta version, then no other revision of "average.cob" can be used to construct an exact copy of the beta release.

Refer to Fig. 8.1. A software system consisting of four modules is ready for beta release. Each module has a different revision level. The first module was easy to produce and required little modification. The third module presented some difficult algorithmic problems. As a result, the third module contains more revisions than any other module. Yet it is the latest revision of all modules that is associated with the beta release. A version label, *beta release"* is associated with each module at the appropriate revision level. Assigning the version label to the latest revision of each module is quite easy as the latest revision contained in an archive file is the default active revision for checking out or administrative commands. To assign the beta release version label to our example files, the PVCS command line would be:

    VCS -v"Beta Release" *.??V

The VCS command is the administrative command. The "-v" option tells VCS that a version label is being assigned. The absence of any specific revision or other version label to associate with the new version label tells the VCS command that the latest revision is to be acted upon. The file specification "*.??V" tells the VCS command to look for archive files in the "VCSDir" directory regardless of the files currently in the local working directory.

As the life cycle continues for a system, more and more versions are released, produced, and required. If tracking of revisions levels associated with various versions was attempted in a way other than the

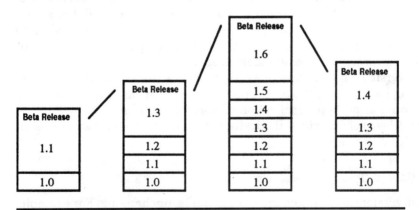

Figure 8.1 Static "beta release" version label.

version label, many "releaseXX.X" files would be required. However, version labels make the problem simple to solve. Refer to Fig. 8.2, in which several versions of the system have been released. Note that by extracting revisions by version label, it is very easy to obtain the correct revisions of all modules in order to build an exact duplicate of any version.

Note also in Fig. 8.2 that any one revision may have more than one version label associated with it. The general rule is that a version label may be associated with one revision and one revision only, whereas any one revision may contain zero or more version labels. The reason for the rule is that a given module may not have changed from one release to another. Only one revision of any module can be associated with a given release. It is impossible for the beta release version to have been constructed with both revisions 1.2 and 1.3 of the same module. It is entirely possible that no revision modification occurred to a module between beta release" and public release 1.0.

When any operation is performed upon an archive file and no revision is specified, the default revision is the tip of the trunk. Unless some method for altering the default revision is present, any work on an alternate development path could present some serious problems. How can a user who is working on branch revisions of multiple archive files keep track of which branches of which archive files are associated with that user's assigned tasks? If all archive files have a branch that extends from the revision associated with the beta release revision, each branch from each archive file could have a completely different major number.

Fortunately, the multiple major number problem has already been solved using a special version label called the floating version label. A

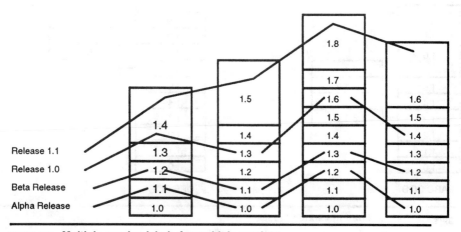

Figure 8.2 Multiple-version labels for multiple versions.

floating version label always "floats" to the tip revision of the branch to which it is assigned. The floating version label can be associated with the configuration parameter "DefaultVersion." The DefaultVersion configuration parameter specifies that the revision associated with the named DefaultVersion version label is to be operated upon by default rather than the tip of the trunk revision.

Refer to Fig. 8.3. Mary is a programmer who is working on a custom release of a software system. Mary will not edit any trunk revisions, she will only edit the revisions associated with the custom release branch. Mary has assigned a floating version label, *Mary's Work*, to each branch associated with the project. She has edited her local configuration file to contain the line, "DefaultVersion = Mary's Work". If she now wishes to edit the tip of the branch associated with the file "ABC.COB", she merely issues the command "get -l ABC.COB" to obtain the correct branch revision.

As Mary continues to work, her floating version label will remain on the tip of the branch. Refer to Fig. 8.4. As Mary checks in revisions, her floating version label will always indicate the tip of the branch that Mary is working on. It does not matter if any other revisions are checked into any other branches or to the trunk, Mary will always be able to obtain the correct revision of whatever file she is working on because of her use of the DefaultVersion configuration parameter and a floating version label.

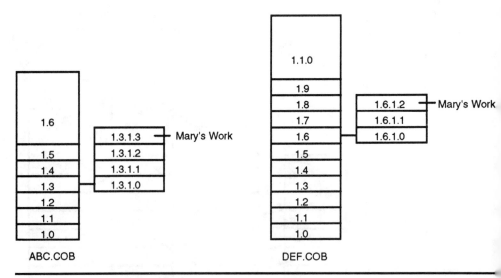

Figure 8.3 Default floating version labels.

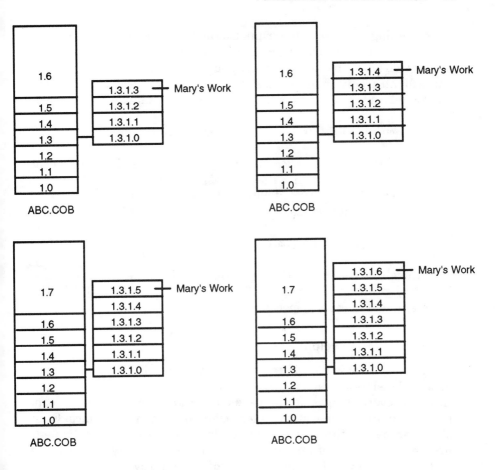

Four Branch Revisions Checked In

Figure 8.4 Floating version label action.

How to Construct a Version

There are several ways to assign version labels to archive files. In general, a version is constructed across a collection of archive files, all of which are in the same state. Usually, the latest revision of the trunk is where the majority of version labels are initially assigned. Naturally, branch development tip revisions are also likely candidates for a version label. However, usually, branches already have some form of version label assigned to them from their inception.

Examining the case of the trunk tip revisions, version labels should be assigned globally, if at all possible. To accomplish global assignment of a version label, the local configuration file should include the VCSDir paths for all archive files to be affected. If this is the case, then a version label can be assigned to all archive files with one simple command:

```
VCS -v"Version Label" *.??V
```

It may be that the normal local configuration file is used for development of a specific group of archive files. In this case, a special local configuration file can be constructed with all the VCSDir paths. In this case, the version label can be assigned to all archive files with the command:

```
VCS -c"Special.cfg" -v"Version Label" *.??V
```

In the above command, the "-c" option specifies the use of a special local configuration file. Instead of using the local "VCS.CFG" file, the command will now use "Special.cfg."

Versions in the Development Process

Version label use is not limited to specific release levels or to floating version labels for branches. As a software system develops, it goes through several stages, initial development, a "test-debug-test" loop, possibly an integration stage, release, and finally, maintenance. Each stage can be identified with a version label. In fact, the development process is simplified if version labels are used to identify the revisions associated with various stages of the software life cycle.

The use of version labels in this context is an extension of the concept of promotion groups. Promotion groups provide a mechanism by which the latest revision of an entire body of code can be assigned a level in the software life cycle. Only those revisions in a development promotion group can be edited. Once promoted beyond the development promotion group, the module cannot be edited. When a module is promoted to the highest promotion group level, it is typically a release level. Identification of the member revisions with a version label is how the exact release level can be identified. Promotion groups do not replace version labels, rather they are an enhancement with the ability to control actions taken upon versions.

Release Control with Version Labels

When a body of code has been tested, verified, and integrated, it is generally released in some form or another. It may be an internal, company-use only release, or it may be a public release of a commercial product. Typically, release numbers are exactly like revision numbers. When the first release of a product is made, it is usually called *Release 1.0*. Whatever the release is called, it is easily identifiable with a version label with the exact same text string. Using a version label to accomplish release tracking makes it very simple to reconstruct exactly the product that was released.

Tracking the Custom Release

Version labels are also a very efficient tool for tracking custom releases of a product or system. Because the version label is a character string, a version can have any name possible with 254 characters. A sample custom release version label may read, *The custom release for Fred Jones and Company made on July 5, 1992.* It may read *Fred Jones 1.1.* Whatever name you wish to apply is a good and legal name as long as it is less than or equal to 254 characters in length. A good rule of thumb, however, is to make the version label succinct so that it is easily remembered and easily entered.

Simplifying the Engineer's Life

Floating version labels, as described above, are a wonder and a blessing for the engineer who is assigned work on an alternative development path. Perhaps the engineer is assigned to a custom release or perhaps to the port to a different platform. Regardless, they are assigned to working on an archive file branch.

No matter how well-controlled the development environment, a given branch will not have the same root revision from one module to the next. In fact, most modules will have a different revision number as the root of the branch. Without floating version labels, the engineer would have to remember (write down on a piece of paper) the branch number for each branch of each revision. However, floating version labels remove this large obstacle to accuracy and performance by freeing the developer of the remembrance task. The developer need merely to establish a DefaultVersion version label and assign that label as a floating version label to each branch or to each revision.

The Quality Assurance Paradigm

Controlling the flow of module revisions through the quality assurance mechanism cannot be over emphasized. Without proper control, the testing organization is testing a moving target. Once a revision is a candidate for testing, it should be promoted into a testing promotion group so that no further editing of the module can take place. The revision so promoted should be identified with a version label that indicates that the revision now belongs to the testing organization. Only when it has been determined that the module contains a bug, should it be demoted to a development promotion group. Once demoted, it should remain so until the next round of promotions for the entire body of code. The testing organization must be able to examine a fixed target to determine if the target is meeting its specifications.

Promotion using promotion groups only may provide insufficient data later when event recreation is required. Several revisions of a single module may receive promotion to test over the development cycle, each is a separate event. Whether or not promotion groups are used, the revision can be promoted from one "version" to another by replacing version labels. For example, replacing the development version label with test promotes the revision from development to test. All modules in the system can be "version label" promoted simultaneously with a single command;

VCS -v"new label"::"old label" *.??V

The double colon syntax tells PVCS to replace "old label" with "new label" in all archive files in the VCSDir paths.

By adding another parameter to the VCS command, promotion groups can be altered as well. For example, to promote a revision from "Test" to "Release" when promotion groups of the same name exist, the command would be:

"VCS -v"new label"::"old label" -g<promotion_group>:"new label" *.??V

In this case, the syntax tells PVCS to assign the promotion group "<promotion group>" to the revision with the "new label" version label. Also in this case, the order of the parameters is important. If the "-g" option was before the "-v" option, the command would fail for all archive files because the "new label" version label has not yet been assigned.

Summary

The version label mechanism is a very powerful tool in two regards: it provides a way to track milestones and releases and it provides a way for programmers to ensure correct revision retrieval without the need for a revision map.

Questions

1. Assume that an emergency bug-fix operation required several modules to be modified. How could you use version labels to simplify the merge of the repaired revisions into a continuing development path?

2. Floating version labels are sometimes called branch version labels. Why? Do you think that this is valid? Why?

9

Fundamentals of Release Management

Controlling the Development Cycle

As a software or other type of system comes into being, it goes through a series of phases until it reaches old age and is retired. These stages are well defined and are known as the software life cycle. At each stage of the life cycle, various documents are created. After their creation, they undergo modifications as both the system as an ideal is mapped to reality and as marketing requirements alter the specifications to appeal to a target audience. As the system matures, it is critical that these documents are updated on a consistent and regular basis to ensure profitability.

In the first phase of a system's life, the system itself is not fully defined, a concept, an idea that needs to be documented to make it become real. Because the system is not fully defined, the documents created to describe it are soon out of date and require modification. The very fundamentals of the idea alter, requirements mature, methods are improved.

Sometimes a new method or requirement proves to be ill-advised. In this case the reasons for failure should be documented to prevent others from falling into the same trap. The basic documents change again to reflect the reversal. Perhaps the ability to retrieve an earlier revision of the document would be useful.

When growth occurs, it is important not only to document the growth, but also to track its changes. An expensive failure can sometimes be easily rectified if revisions of design, requirements, and specification documents are stored under configuration management. These documents and many more, including manuals, guides, data sheets, and any other document type associated with the product are all a part of the overall system. The most important document type is, of course, source code. But source code does not the product make. A wonderful application with no packaging, poor documentation, or any other of a number of potential deficiencies may as well be no application at all.

All forms of documentation, from specification to source code and all stops in between, must be consistent. The application should adhere to the specification. The user documentation should adhere to the specification. The common ground for all components of a product is the specification. The specification should adhere to the requirements. If alteration of requirement or specification occurs, it is important that all concerned personnel have access to the new revision of the document. All too often, engineering manufactures a product that adheres to a specification that is out of date. It is not engineering's fault that the specification was modified six months into a seven month development schedule. Or was it that engineering was notified in month six of a specification change that happened in month three and that if engineering had been notified in month three, the product would have complied?

If specifications and requirements documents are stored under version control, then it is very easy for a user to determine if the copy of a document that they currently have is out of date or not. If it is out of date, they can obtain the new revision immediately. They can find out exactly how the document changed by using the "VDIFF" command. They can then turn around and implement those changes in a much more efficient manner. After all, they know exactly what the changes were. They don't have to hunt for them by pouring over the document in detail, trying to mentally detect and remember the differences.

Documentation groups benefit in the same way. Exact differences can be determined. If change bars are not available, the reviewer can request a listing of the exact differences. The author can verify their changes. Custom modifications can be stored. "Did I change that paragraph on the transcendence of paraphysical electron excitation?" Multiple versions for multiple platforms or custom releases can be stored. "You need a copy of the custom manual we made for who? Oh, just a minute, I'll check out the correct branch for you."

Hopefully, the testing organization has been part of or privy to the design of the product. If the environment is ideal, the testing team is producing test plans while the design team is producing specifications and, possibly, pseudocode. Test cases are produced. Test programs are designed and implemented. Test data files are constructed. Test data and programs are developed, they change over time. The changes to test documentation, programs, and data are just as important to track as the source code is. The testing organization is a entity by whom all other aspects are measured. If testing is invalid, so is the product.

Any document relating in any way to the system, that is subject to change, should be under the control of the configuration management system.

Quality Control, Revisited

As the system reaches maturity, it begins to comply with the specification in a measurable manner. In the case of a computer program, more and more of the source code modules are achieving functionality. Eventually, the system is integrated and a running program produced. Development works out all the wrinkles that it can find and declares that the system is ready for test. Of course, testing will find bugs. Development then fixes them. It is here, at this adolescent phase of the system's life, that the system is made or broken.

No matter the quality and precision of the testing organizations battery of examinations, if the system is not controlled, it will transcend an enjoyable middle age and enter into the maintenance phase forever. Some companies have reported that the maintenance costs of a system accounted for over eighty percent of the cost of the entire system. Why? Someone knows, but is not talking. After all, it would be hard to admit that all those releases were for bug fixes. It is much easier to say that a continual upgrade process with constant product improvement makes for a market leader.

The reason the product enters the maintenance phase so soon is not because of poor design, sloppy algorithms, or stupidity on any person's part. Everyone on the team, developer, tester, manager or whomever, has the same goal. That goal is to have a good product out the door on schedule. There is a common bond that is sometimes overlooked as development points a finger at test who points a finger back. If the system had been under control, no finger pointing would have been called for.

In many cases, poor product performance or poor compliance with the specification can be attributed to the lack of control of the system during the test-fix-test loop. Refer to Fig. 9.1. Shortly after the test cycle commenced, a bug was found and reported to the development organization. The development organization jumped right on it and within just a few days had a fix. The fix was handed over to test who quickly verified that it passed and then continued the test cycle. The question is, when test found a new bug several days later, was that new bug an old bug or a bug resulting from the bug fix? There is no way to tell.

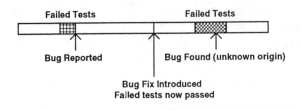

Figure 9.1   Standard test-fix-test loop with consequences.

Now refer to Fig. 9.2. When the same first bug was found by test, they reported it to development. Development fixed it within a few days. However, the fix was not folded back into the test bed. Testing continued until the entire test cycle was completed and all bugs identified. When development believes that it has repaired all known bugs, a new test cycle begins. The repair of old bugs is verified and any new bugs are reported. This test-fix-test cycle reoccurs until all tests are passed. The product is a known entity. It complies with the specification. It works. If the tests were well conceived, the product should enjoy a mellow middle age interrupted only by enhancements.

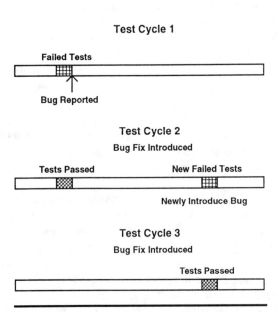

Figure 9.2   Improved test-fix-test loop with configuration management.

Configuration Management using PVCS provides two tools for the control of the system in the adolescent stage. These two tools are promotion groups and version labels.

Promotion Groups

As a software system matures, it traverses the seven phases of the software life cycle. Of these phases, the most rapid growth occurs during the implementation, integration, test, posttest, and release phases. During implementation, the system is a collection of parts. During integration, the parts begin to work as a system. During test, the system is verified. During posttest, the testing is verified. Finally, at release, the system graduates into customer usefulness.

If the growth phases are grouped together, then they can be classified. The implementation and integration phases could be said to belong in the development promotion group. The test and posttest phases could be said to belong to the quality control promotion group. When construed as a collection of promotion groups, it becomes easy to apply rules of conduct to each group that may or may not apply to other groups and to enforce those rules. For example, a revision of a module that is a member of a development promotion group can be created and modified. Once that revision graduates into the test promotion group, or any other promotion group higher in priority, it can no longer be edited. Because rules can be applied to a promotion group, establishing a promotion group definition can enable application of rules to revisions depending upon promotion group membership.

PVCS provides promotion group control functionality. A software development organization can be analyzed and groups defined. More often than not, the software system under construction is composed of a number of subsystems. If desired, each subsystem can be defined in a unique development promotion group. Refer to Fig. 9.3. Whatever the composition of the organization, groups can be defined to mirror that composition. *Development groups* are defined as one or more development promotion groups. The development promotion group is the lowest level of group. If *test* is the next higher promotion group level defined, then modules are promoted from the development promotion group to the test promotion group. Revisions in the development promotion group may be altered. Once promoted beyond development, a revision may not be altered. Once a revision is promoted to *test*, the revision remains constant unless it is demoted because of test failure. If it passes all tests the revision may then graduate from the "test" promotion group to the *beta test* promotion group or even on to *release* or *production* or whatever name has been applied to the next promotion

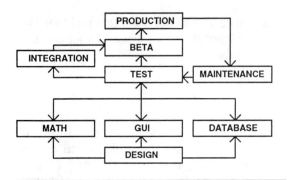

Figure 9.3 Potential promotion groups with promotion/demotion paths.

group level. The PVCS promotion hierarchy is completely user definable on a project-by-project basis.

Once a revision of a module is ready for graduation, it is promoted into the next higher level of group. The trend toward a higher promotion group continues until the revision has attained the highest level. When this occurs, the revision should be identified with a version label that references the release name or number to which it belongs.

Version Labels

Promotion groups are used for current work in progress. However, they do not permanently identify revisions as a part of a given release. Once a system has been released, it often is enhanced. When it is enhanced, the enhancement project reuses the promotion group definitions. The original release revision is not now identified unless version labels have been used to identify the release that the revision is associated with.

Refer to Fig. 9.4. A single module is used to represent all modules in the system. Each module contains the exact same version labels even though the number of revisions may differ drastically from one module to the next. The initial version label is virtual, that is, it is not physically assigned to any revision. The initial version label in our example is "development." By default, the last revision checked into the trunk of an archive file is the "development" trunk revision. The "development" virtual version label is a floating version label and remains at the top of the archive revision tree. When the revision attains its first promotion to test, the default virtual version label is replaced with a real "test" version label. This particular revision contained a bug, so a new "development" version revision was created. When the "test" revision achieves functionality, it is then promoted to

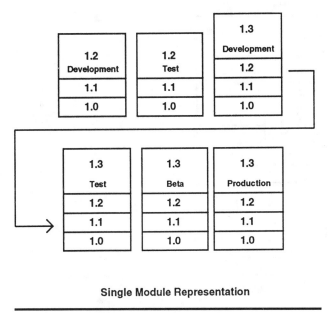

Single Module Representation

Figure 9.4   Version label promotion method.

"Alpha", or perhaps "Beta Test" and the "test" version label replaced with, in our case, "Beta." Finally, the "Beta" version revision is promoted to "Release 1.0".

Tracking Releases

After Release 1.0 has been in use for a time, usually a change request or an enhancement request will cause the generation of a new development cycle for the system. In Fig. 9.5, the representative module has been altered to implement a requested enhancement. A new development version revision has been created. Note that the revision associated with Release 1.0 is still identified by a version label, even though a newer development revision that is part of a development promotion group has been added. Again, the development version revision is promoted to the test version as a member of the test promotion group, on to beta as a member of the appropriate promotion group, and finally Release 2.0. as a member of the production promotion group.

Each time a new release of the software system is made, it can be identified with a fixed version label that specifies the name of the release. Whether the release is called Release 1.0 or Banana does not matter. Naturally, a name that has some bearing on the described subject will be far easier to remember thirty-six months from now.

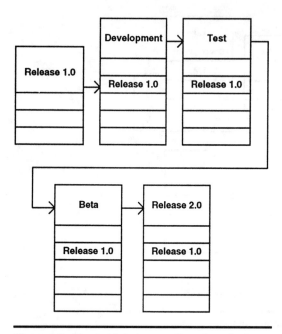

Figure 9.5   Version label promotion of product enhancement release.

Using a Single Database

When all revisions of all modules are stored in a single database, the entire life of the system can be readily identified. However, there may be drawbacks. One problem is that along with vital revisions, questionable revisions exist. For example, in Fig. 9.6, a module with over thirty revisions is evaluated. Only four revisions have version labels. By examining the change descriptions, it is determined that twenty-six revisions were the result of bug fixes or syntax errors. Most of these

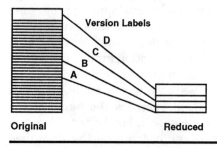

Figure 9.6   Archive file size reduction.

revisions are of questionable value and most occur before the first version-labeled revision. While this is completely acceptable, it may be that storage space is at a premium or that several years have passed and no one cares about those questionable revisions. For whatever reason, if the questionable revisions are to be deleted, they must be carefully deleted by hand.

A Two-Database System

Using a dual-database system, most of the maintenance problems associated with long term storage are alleviated. The mechanism automatically deletes questionable revisions by default. Here is how it works.

When a system under control of a development database is first promoted to release or production level, the revisions associated with that revision are checked in, with an identifying version label, as the initial revision in a second database, called the *release database*. The original database is then archived for future reference, if needed. When an enhancement or modification request is made, either the original development database is restored or, more likely, a new development database is formed using the latest revision from the release database. Once the enhanced system is ready for promotion to production or release, the proper revisions are checked into the release database with an appropriate identifying version label.

Using the dual-database system, all major versions of a system can be maintained while the development database is recreated over and over again. The release database does not contain any syntax error revisions, or for that matter, any other questionable revision. The questionable revisions are archived, not in the release database, but in the form of a backup of the development database to disk or tape. The revisions can be recovered if needed, but the need to do so would surely come but rarely.

Interfacing to the Mainframe

An effective implementation of the dual-database system is realized when network development is targeted at a mainframe computer. Typically, a mainframe computer will have its own system for revision control. The paradigm of checking "release" or "production" revisions into a second database is realized by uploading those same revisions to a mainframe and checking them into the mainframe's own revision control system.

The PVCS series of products includes a library gateway that provides transparent access to host libraries and PVCS LAN-based libraries. The "PVCS Production GateWay" automatically integrates configuration management capabilities on the LAN with host-based library management systems. It is not within the scope of this book to discuss the use of this tool beyond the fact that integration of LAN-based development with mainframe systems is a powerful, economical solution to the problems inherent with downsizing.

Summary

The primary tool in release management and tracking is the version label. Regardless of whether multiple archive file databases are in use or a single archive file database, the key to identification of a specific release is the version label assigned to the revisions in all the modules that correspond to the release.

Questions

1. Why is it so important to track releases?

2. Why is it important to be able to reconstruct a release even after the release has been superseded?

3. Can you think of a way to track releases without version labels? Does it require the creation of a file in which to store the data?

4. What weakness is there in the use of version labels to track releases? What strengths?

10

Setting up and Configuring PVCS

Setting PVCS up is a straightforward and simple process. The first step is to install the programs. Refer to Fig. 10.1. For network installations, the standard executable programs should be located in a directory to which every PVCS user has read and execute privileges. The administrative programs should be placed in a directory with access limited to system administration and management personnel. Two of the most important programs to safeguard are "vconfig.exe" and "makedb.exe." It is these two programs that provide, establish and maintain the PVCS security system.

After the programs have been installed, the next step is to configure the executable programs. Configuration is accomplished with the

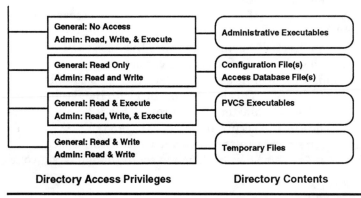

Directory Access Privileges	Directory Contents
General: No Access Admin: Read, Write, & Execute	Administrative Executables
General: Read Only Admin: Read and Write	Configuration File(s) Access Database File(s)
General: Read & Execute Admin: Read, Write, & Execute	PVCS Executables
General: Read & Write Admin: Read & Write	Temporary Files

Figure 10.1 Suggested PVCS directories access rights and contents.

"vconfig.exe" program. The "vconfig.exe" program is used for establishing the level of security, the method of user identification, and other pertinent data. The "vconfig.exe" program embeds this information permanently into each and every PVCS executable. Once these install time configuration parameters have been set using "vconfig.exe", the only way to alter them is to again use "vconfig.exe". It is because of the ability of "vconfig.exe" to modify the actual executables to remove or alter established security that the "vconfig.exe" program should not be accessible by the general user.

The "makedb.exe" program should also be kept under tight access control because it is this program that establishes user and group definitions, permissions, and restrictions. Naturally, the text input file used by "makedb.exe" to produce the encrypted enhanced access control database should be kept under lock and key.

Install Time Configuration

Once the installation of the PVCS programs has been completed, it is time to customize the applications for the environment in which they will run. At this time, several decisions will have to be made. First, will a Master Configuration File be used? If so, where will it be stored? (Usually it is stored in a directory in which the general user has read only privileges.)

Using a Master Configuration File provides the ability to establish guidelines and performance criteria that cannot be altered by the general user. Recall that one of the Master Configuration file parameters is Disallow. The Disallow parameter provides a mechanism by which established parameters can be "set in concrete."

If PVCS is to be used in secure mode, it is essential that a Master Configuration file be used. There are several parameters, including AccessDB that should not be alterable by the general user. Imagine the problems that would arise if a carefully constructed access control database could be bypassed because a general user discovers that AccessDB can be redirected. Fortunately, once the AccessDB parameter has been disallowed, the circumvention cannot occur.

If a Master Configuration file is used, then each PVCS executable needs to be made aware of this fact. This is accomplished with the "vconfig.exe" program. Assume that the Master Configuration file is named "Master.CFG" and resides in the secure directory "H:\bin\PVCS\Admin". Change working directories to that in which the PVCS executables reside, in this case "H:\bin\PVCS". Then execute the following command line:

VCONFIG -cH:\bin\PVCS\Admin\Master.CFG *.exe

VCONFIG -cH:\bin\PVCS\Admin\Master.CFG *.dll

The "-c" option tells "vconfig.exe" that all command line characters after the "c" up to the first blank character represent the path and file name for the Master Configuration File. Once this command has been issued, all PVCS programs will attempt to read "H:\bin\PVCS\admin\Master.CFG". If a PVCS program fails to read this file for any reason, it will terminate immediately.

The "vconfig.exe" program stores information in the header of the PVCS executables. Each executable in the working directory is examined to determine whether or not it is a PVCS executable. If it is not, a message appears on the screen stating that the examined program, mentioned by name, is not configurable and that the program is not altered in any fashion. If, however, the examined program is a PVCS executable, then the program header is modified. Refer to Fig. 10.2. The program header illustrated on the left has not been modified and

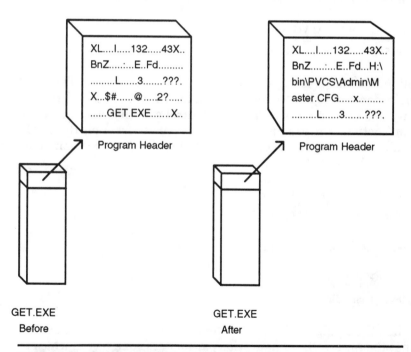

Figure 10.2   Affect on GET.EXE program header after running
"vconfig-ch:\bin\PVCS\Admin\Master.Cfg GET.EXE"

contains programmatic information not meant for human use. The program header on the right has been modified and now contains a reference to the Master Configuration file.

The next decision to be made is whether or not to use enhanced access control security. In most cases, the decision is not very difficult or long in coming. Yes, implement enhanced access control security. Note that enabling enhanced access control security implies that an access control database will be created using "makedb.exe". To enable the enhanced access control security feature, ensure that the current working directory contains the PVCS executables and issue the commands:

"VCONFIG -s *.exe"

"VCONFIG -s *.dll"

It is not necessary to change working directories to the directory that contains the PVCS executables if the full path is included in the command line. For example, from any directory, (and assuming that the PVCS executables "live" in the directory "H:\bin\PVCS"), the same effect can be achieved by issuing the commands:

"VCONFIG -s H:\bin\PVCS*.exe"

"VCONFIG -s H:\bin\PVCS*.dll"

Optionally, the "vconfig.exe" option "-sy" can be used. The "-sy" option is identical to the "-s" option. Both turn enhanced access control security on. To turn enhanced access control security off, simply use the "-sn" option. For example, to remove security from all the PVCS executables residing in the directory "H:\bin\PVCS," the commands issued would be:

"VCONFIG -sn H:\bin\PVCS*.exe"

"VCONFIG -sn H:\bin\PVCS*.dll"

or, issuing the commands from the H:\bin\PVCS directory:

"VCONFIG -sn *.exe"

"VCONFIG -sn *.dll"

Earlier, the configuration parameter AccessDB was mentioned. Recall that the AccessDB configuration parameter is one way in which to tell any and all PVCS commands the name and location of the access control database file. However, the AccessDB method mandates the use of a Master Configuration file. Another method that can be used with or without a Master Configuration file is an install time option to "vconfig.exe". Using the install time option ensures that all PVCS programs will behave identically and that the access control database file cannot be circumvented easily. In fact, it cannot be circumvented at all if a Master Configuration file is used and the configuration parameter Disallow is applied to the configuration parameter AccessDB.

The directory where the access control database file is found depends upon how the users are identified and whether or not they will be allowed to alter their passwords. If the user's password is defined in the access control database file and the user is to be allowed to alter his or her password, then the access control database file must reside in a directory in which the user has read and write privileges. If the user identification is accomplished from the network login, then the user's network password is used to establish identification and the password feature of the enhanced access control database is not required. In this case, the enhanced access control database file should be maintained in a directory in which the general user has only read privileges. If the user's password is stored in the enhanced access control database and the ability to change the password is required, the user must have write privileges. This also means that a user can delete the file!

In most networks, the user identification is accomplished when the user logs into the network. In this case, the user password is network based rather than enhanced access control database based, and the enhanced access control database file should be stored in a secure directory.

To permanently embed the path and name of the access control database file into PVCS executables, the "-a" option to the "vconfig.exe" program is used. As in the "-c" option, "vconfig.exe" will embed all characters following the "a" in the "-a" option up to but not including the next space encountered on the command line.

If we assume that the access control database file is named "access.db" and resides in the directory "H:\bin\PVSC\Admin," then the command lines that will embed the path and file names into the PVCS executables when the current working directory contains those executables are:

"VCONFIG -aH:\bin\PVSC\Admin\access.db *.exe"

"VCONFIG -aH:\bin\PVSC\Admin\access.db *.dll"

The final application of "vconfig.exe" is to embed the source from which PVCS commands are to determine the user identification. If PVCS is to be used on a stand-alone personal computer (not connected to the network) then the "vlogin.exe" program should be used to insure the user's identity. In this case, the enhanced access control database password facility is used. If, however, the workstation is attached to a network, then the user identification can be obtained from the network. The assumption here is that if the user is on the network, he or she must have known his or her own password and are thus valid users.

The "-i" option to the "vconfig.exe" program is used to establish the source for the user identification. Refer to Table 10.1. PVCS provides a number of predefined sources. For the purposes of this discussion, assume that the workstations are connected via a Novell network running Novell's "Netware". To embed this information into the PVCS executables, issue the following commands:

VCONFIG -iNETWARE *.exe

VCONFIG -iNETWARE *.dll

In general, the "-i" option to "vconfig.exe" is used as follows to indicate the source for user identification, where source is one of the selections from Table 10.1:

VCONFIG -iSOURCE *.exe

VCONFIG -iSOURCE *.dll

TABLE 10.1   "VCONFIG.EXT" Identification Sources

SOURCE	Description
HOST	Host operating system. UNIX or multi-network environments.
LANMAN	IBM LAN Manager for DOS and OS/2
NETWARE	Novell NetWare for DOS and OS/2
3PLUS	3Com 3+ network for DOS
VCSID	Local environmental variable. NOT SECURE!
VLOGIN	"vlogin.exe" terminate and stay resident program for DOS.
UNKNOWN	No SOURCE. If used, prevents access violation errors.

At any time, all settings made to PVCS executables using the "vconfig.exe" program may be removed or "undone" with the "-u" option. For example, to return all PVCS executables in the directory "H:\bin\PVCS" to their default condition, issue the following commands:

VCONFIG -u *.exe

VCONFIG -u *.dll

The "vconfig.exe" program provides an easy to use and powerful mechanism with which to alter the characteristics and performance of PVCS executables with a one-time-only "shot in the arm." Once the PVCS executables have been configured using "vconfig.exe," they remain so. There is no need to maintain a special file with PVCS configuration information. If, at any time, the need arises to determine how the PVCS executables are configured, the "vconfig.exe" program again comes into use. This time, however, no parameters are passed and only one file should be referenced. Note that you can reference all programs in the directory if you desire. However, because they are all configured identically, the screen of your computer will fill and scroll by with the same information over and over again. It is redundant information, at least it should be if all PVCS executables were configured in the same way. To determine the common configuration settings, issue the command:

"VCONFIG get.exe"

where "get.exe" could easily be replaced with any of the other PVCS program names.

Converting Old Archives

If an older version (preversion 3.1) of PVCS is already in use and the installation is an upgrade, the older archive files must be converted to the new style if enhanced access control is to be used. The conversion is accomplished with the "vconfig.exe" program. Instead of turning security on for PVCS executables, the "vconfig.exe" program converts older archives when archive files are referenced rather than executables. If an old archive file "myfile.c_v" was created using version 3.0 of PVCS, the archive file can be upgraded to accept enhanced access control by issuing the command:

VCONFIG -s myfile.c_v

or optionally:

VCONFIG -sy myfile.c_v

PVCS Configuration

All PVCS commands use configuration files to learn what their expected behavior under given circumstances should be. A configuration file is an ASCII file that contains configuration parameters. In addition, conditional constructs can be included so that on-the-fly decisions can be made based upon the outcome of a logical statement. The configuration parameters define the operation of the PVCS system. Conditional constructs provide flexibility and adaptability to a variety of situations. A configuration file can be used to "call" other configuration files as well. The configuration parameter used to call on other configuration files is "@<filename>". Alternate configuration files may be nested up to twenty levels deep.

Configuration Parameters

There are three types of configuration parameters. Recall that *archive attributes* are parameters that define qualities to be attached to an archive file when it is created. After the archive file has been created, these qualities may be altered using the administrative command "VCS". Some examples of archive attributes are AccessList, (who or what groups can access the file?), Compress, (how much compression, if any, is to be used on the file?), and ExpandKeywords, (are keywords found within the file to be expanded?).

The second type of configuration parameter is the *action declaration*. These parameters tell PVCS what to do under certain circumstances, what directories to perform the work in, whether or not to make audit trail file entries, where to put temporary files, and many more actions. Some of these parameters will have an impact upon performance (in terms of speed) if set incorrectly. For example, if a network server has a large disk, (call it "E:"), and a RAM disk, (call it "F:") and a workstation connected to the network has a hard disk, (call it "C:"), then the setting of the configuration parameter WorkDir can be very important. If WorkDir is set to "C:\TEMP", then multiple network transfers will occur during a file operation and performance will suffer. If WorkDir is set to "E:\PVCSWORK", then less transfer time will be required and the performance will improve. If, however, WorkDir is set to "F:\FASTTEMP", then the best possible performance will be realized because a RAM disk is far faster than is a standard hard disk. (Be sure that the RAM disk is large enough to accept the files.)

The third type of configuration parameter is used to make decisions based upon the suffix of the workfile. For example, if the Log keyword is contained in the workfile, then a user's change comments will be inserted into the file when any new revision is checked in. It would not do any good to have a "/*" character sequence inserted as a comment delimiter in a FORTRAN file. Nor would "C" work in a C language file. Yet it may well be that an organization works with both computer languages and has an assortment of source code files with ".FOR" and ".C" file suffixes. Using the "CommentPrefix.<ext>" configuration parameter, the comment delimiter for different types of files can be differentiated. In the above example, the following configuration parameter lines in a configuration file would differentiate the comment delimiters for the two file types:

CommentPrefix.C="/* "CommentPrefix.FOR="C "

In another example, it may be that there is little free space left on the disk volume that stores COBOL files and significant free space on the disk volume that stores test files. If the test files have a ".DAT" suffix, then it is possible to apply compression to the COBOL files while leaving the ".DAT" files in their native archive file format. The configuration file specification would be as follows:

Compress.COB
NoCompress.DAT

Conditional Constructs

A *conditional construct* can be used to provide a mechanism by which alternatives are considered and one chosen based upon the outcome of a simple true or false question. The decision may be based upon the presence of a special file or directory. The decision may be based upon whether an alias or environmental variable has been set, and if so, what the setting is. The decision may be based upon the comparison of two items.

Refer to Fig. 10.3. There are two "if" constructs wherein an expression is evaluated to determine a course of action. An expression is a

```
%if <expression>
      <configuration parameter>

   %elseif <expression>
         <configuration parameter>

   %else
         <configuration parameter>
   %endif
%endif
```

Figure 10.3   Form for conditional constructs.

logical statement that will evaluate to either true of false. If the statement evaluates as true, then the configuration parameters immediately following the "%if" statement will be issued. If the outcome of the evaluation is false, then if an "%else" statement is present, the configuration parameters following the "%else" will be invoked. There is no requirement that an "%if" statement be followed by "%else". Each "%if" or "%elseif" statement must be concluded with a "%endif," (or "%end"), statement.

The outcome of an expression can be controlled or directed using operators. Operators can also be used to construct the expression. Figure 10.4 lists the operators in their order of precedence. Using the operators, it is easy to construct comparison expressions. For example, the expression "%if !("FRED" == "$(VCSID)" will evaluate to true if the user does not have a login name of "FRED".

PVCS also provides some special expressions called conditional keywords. These special expressions, illustrated in Fig. 10.5, provide a mechanism by which complex expressions can be constructed that would otherwise be nearly impossible to implement. A conditional keyword will evaluate to true if the referenced item exists or has been defined.

A conditional construct that tests to see if an environmental variable "PROJECT" has been defined and then makes decisions based upon the setting of that environmental variable is illustrated in Fig. 10.6. The conditional construct is well-behaved in that it will inform the user about any problems that are encountered during processing and will tell the user how to correct the situation. If an error is encountered, the PVCS command will abort, or stop, after giving the user a message. The illustrated conditional construct uses DOS conventions. Naturally, if PVCS is running under a different operating system, some changes may need to be made in the syntax. For example, the "\" character is DOS specific, under UNIX, the "/" character would be substituted.

!	Logical Negation
<	Less than
>	Greater than
>=	Greater than or equal to
<=	Less than or equal to
= or ==	Equal
!= or <>	Not equal
& or &&	Logical conjunction (AND)
^ or ^^	Logical exclusion (XOR)
I or II	Logical disjunction (OR)

Figure 10.4 Conditional construct operators.

%Exists (<filename> or <directory name>)

%File (<filename>)

%Dir (<directory name>)

%Defined (<alias> or <environmental variable>)

Figure 10.5   Conditional expression conditional keywords.

```
%if   %Defined $(PROJECT)

    %if  ("$(PROJECT)" =="DIAGS" II "$(PROJECT)"=="DATABASE")

        VCSDIR=H:\PROJECTS\VCS\$(PROJECT)\*
        @H:\PROJECTS\CFG\$(PROJECT).CFG
        ACCESSDB=H:\PROJECTS\ADMIN\$(PROJECT).ADB
        JOURNAL=H:\PROJECTS\ADMIN\$(PROJECT).JNL
        %elseif ("$(PROJECT)" =="FINANCIALS" II "$(PROJECT)"=="AMORT"
            VCSDIR=G:\BANKING\$(PROJECT)\vcs\*
            @G:\BANKING\$(PROJECT)\$(PROJECT).CFG
            ACCESSDB=H:\BANKING\$(PROJECT)\$(PROJECT).ADB
            %elseif %Exists D:\$(PROJECT).CFG
                @D:\$(PROJECT).CFG
            %else
                ECHO INVALID PROJECT, $(PROJECT),  DEFINED
                ECHO Please reset PROJECT and try again.
                ABORT

        %endif

    %endif

%endif
%else
    ECHO ERROR: NO PROJECT DEFINED
    ECHO Exiting.......
    ABORT
%endif

DISALLOW ACCESSDB LOGIN VCSDIR JOURNAL
```

Figure 10.6   Conditional construct example.

When used correctly, conditional constructs and file suffix based decision parameters give PVCS tremendous flexibility and the ability to adapt to many situations on the fly with no user interaction or specification required. Along with such freedom and power, comes the need to ensure that the configuration files and parameters are really the ones that are desired. With that need comes the responsibility to learn about and understand the various parameters and how they affect day-to-day activities.

Run-Time Configuration

Run-time configuration is the establishing of the settings for configuration parameters based upon information contained in configuration files when a PVCS application is running.

When any PVCS command is issued, the invoked program will look for configuration information. The program follows a distinct course of action when seeking configuration information. The first place that the PVCS program will find such information is the Master Configuration File. Naturally, if the install time configuration was not used to establish a Master Configuration File, one will not be sought.

Within the Master Configuration File, references may be made to additional configuration files. The invoked PVCS program will read these additional configuration files before completing processing of the Master Configuration File.

Once the PVCS program has completed processing the Master Configuration File, it checks the command line that was used for the invocation to see if the "-c<configuration file name>" option was used. If so, the program then reads "<configuration file name>" for further configuration information. The file "<configuration file name>" may also call other configuration files with the "@<filename>" configuration parameter.

If the invoked PVCS program does not find a command line configuration file parameter, the PVCS program looks in the current working directory for a file named "vcs.cfg". In this case, it is said that PVCS is reading a local configuration file. The local configuration file may also call other configuration files using the "@<filename>" configuration parameter.

If no command line directive was found and no local configuration file was found, the invoked PVCS program then examines the environmental variable table to determine if an environmental variable, *VCSCFG,* is defined. The VCSCFG environmental variable may be set at boot time through a startup file such as "autoexec.bat" under DOS, or it may be set by the user at another time using the "set environmental variable" command appropriate for the operating system in use. The environmental configuration file may also call other configuration files.

The run time configuration file evaluation is illustrated as a flow chart in Fig. 10.7. When processing of all configuration files is complete, the invoked PVCS program then evaluates the security requirements, reading the access control database (if any) and determining the user name and permissions prior to performing any action upon any source or archive files.

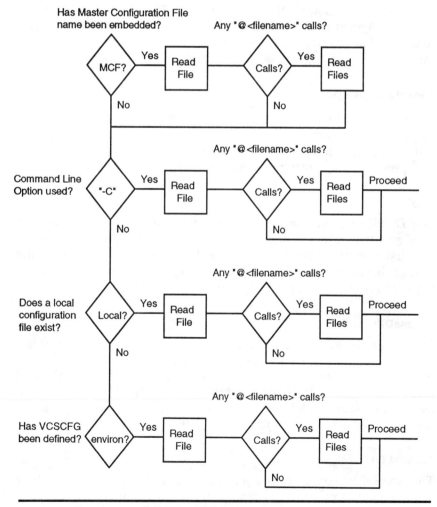

Figure 10.7   Run time configuration flowchart.

The Master Configuration File

The Master Configuration File is the most powerful of the configuration files. A small subset of special configuration parameters can only be used in the Master Configuration File (There are some other configuration parameters that should only be used in the Master Configuration File). These special configuration parameters include, AccessDB, Disallow, EndMaster, and Login. Two of these parameters, AccessDB and Login override the information embedded into PVCS executables at install time. Because these two parameters are critical to accurate and efficient security, they should not be altered by users. To prevent alteration, and thus the defeat of these two parameters, they can be disallowed. Refer back to Fig. 10.6, in which these and other configuration parameters are disallowed using the Disallow configuration parameter. Once a parameter has been disallowed, it cannot be changed by any user.

Important Decisions

Some of the configuration parameters have far-reaching consequences if they are not used correctly. While it is not within the scope of this book to address all the configuration parameters, those whose impact may be unexpected or may cause consternation and confusion are discussed.

Disallow

The *Disallow configuration parameter* is used only in the Master Configuration File. The Disallow configuration parameter is followed by a list of configuration parameters that will be locked, that is, not changeable by any user. The Disallow configuration parameter is a key ingredient in both security and policy enforcement.

AccessDB

The *AccessDB configuration parameter* is used to name the access control database file. As discussed earlier, the AccessDB configuration parameter overrides the access control database file name embedded into PVCS executables during install time configuration. It would not be a very good idea to let user's name their own access control database files, therefore, it is a good idea to disallow the parameter.

AccessList

The *AccessList configuration parameter* is an archive file attribute parameter that will be inherited by any newly created archive files. If users are allowed to create archive files and it is not desired that the user be the one to specify access rights to those files, then the AccessList configuration parameter should be set and then disallowed in the Master Configuration File.

AutoCreate

The *AutoCreate configuration parameter* tells PVCS that if, during a check-in operation, (PUT command), an archive file for the subject source file cannot be found, then the check-in operation is to create an archive file for the source file. This configuration parameter can be very, very dangerous. For example, recall that the VCSDir (directory path for archive files) for a user is contained in his or her local configuration file. The reason for this is that the user works on several projects and is constantly requiring a new VCSDir setting. Rather than mandate the VCSDir setting in the Master Configuration File, the user has several local configuration files in several directories, each with a different VCSDir setting. The user need merely change working directories to work on a new or different project. If, for some reason, the user copies a file from one directory to another for whatever reason, and then edits the file, there is a risk of an inadvertent archive file creation. If the user does not copy the file back into the correct directory, then change working directory to that correct directory, before they invoke a check-in (PUT), then an error will surely occur. If the (incorrect) working directory does not have a local configuration file that specifies the correct VCS directory, and the user attempts to check in a new revision of the file from that directory, then PVCS will not be able to find the existing archive file and will create a new one with a single revision. If our user is paying attention, then he or she may notice that he or she is entering a file description rather than a change description. Notice the word "if!"

Another potential problem with the AutoCreate configuration parameter is that an archive file might be created in an unexpected directory. For example, if a user creates a new file and then checks it in, the archive file for that source file will be created in the first directory in the VCSDir path. If the user has a definite destination directory in mind, then they must specify it on the command line. If he or she forgets to do so, then the archive file is created in the first VCSDir directory. If, however, under the same scenario, the active configuration parameter is NoAutoCreate, then the user's command to check in the new file would fail because the archive file does not yet exist. The user would be forced to create the file specifically, using the "VCS -i" command. Because a *special* command is required, the user is much more apt to remember to specify the correct path for the archive file. The recommendation? Set NoAutoCreate and then Disallow AutoCreate.

CheckLock

The *CheckLock configuration parameter* ensures that the person who is checking in a new revision of a module is the person who owns the archive file lock. When a user checks out a module for modification, the PVCS system locks the appropriate revision with the user identification of the user. If NoCheckLock is the active configuration parameter, then any user may check in a new revision. The recommendation is to set CheckLock in the Master Configuration File and then disallow resetting of the parameter using Disallow CheckLock or Disallow NoCheckLock. Either way, the same goal is accomplished. It does not matter if the configuration parameter or its negative is disallowed.

ExpandKeywords

The *ExpandKeywords configuration parameter* tells the PVCS "PUT" command to expand keywords contained in the module. For example, the keyword $Revision$ would expand to $Revision: 1.0$ when the module is first checked in.

Some programs, in particular word processors, do not store their data files in a linear format. Instead, blocks are stored with identifiers that tell the word processor how to construct the document from the blocks. The identifiers contain a byte count of the length of the block. If a keyword is expanded, the actual byte count increases while the stored byte count does not. The next time the application attempts to open the file, it will fail to read it correctly and present the user with garbage. In the case where one of these type applications is in use, there are two solutions to the expansion problem, force a fixed number of characters in the keyword expansion or set the NoExpandKeywords configuration parameter.

The ExpandKeywords configuration parameter can also specify file types. This facility makes it easy to protect sensitive documents while using the valuable keywords in other files. For example:

```
ExpandKeywords .c .cob .for
NoExpandKeywords .doc
```

FirstMatch

The *FirstMatch configuration parameter* is used to tell all PVCS commands to stop their directory search for a file if other files of the same type, (file suffix), are found in a directory. Using FirstMatch mandates that all files of any given type reside in the same directory. While this may not be a burden upon a small development task, it is probably better to establish a functional hierarchy of files rather than a hierarchy based upon the file type.

ExclusiveLock

The *ExclusiveLock configuration parameter* specifies that only one lock may exist in an archive file. If one user locks the trunk tip revision for editing, no other user may lock any other revision for any reason. If parallel development occurs, the user who wishes to edit a branch revision would not be able to do so if a revision on the trunk were locked. The ExclusiveLock configuration parameter prohibits the parallel development paradigm.

MultiLock

The *MultiLock [revision or user] configuration parameter* is the opposite of the ExclusiveLock configuration parameter, and as such, the two are mutually exclusive. The MultiLock configuration parameter allows a single user to lock multiple revisions of a single archive file. The MultiLock configuration parameter also allows multiple users to lock the same revision of an archive file. The "MultiLock REVISION" setting allows more than one user to lock a revision but prohibits any one user from owning more than one lock in the archive file. The MultiLock USER setting allows a single user to own multiple locks in an archive but only one lock of any one revision. The MultiLock configuration parameter has no effect on an archive file that was created when the ExclusiveLock configuration parameter was in effect.

Use of the MultiLock configuration parameter should be consistent from one user to another. It is recommended that the MultiLock configuration parameter be established and then disallowed in the Master Configuration File.

Journal

The *Journal configuration parameter* must be used if an audit trail is desired. An audit trail is an invaluable tool for engineers and other developers as an aide to debugging and module life cycle tracking. Also, managers will find an audit trail to be useful in producing project reports. Through the audit trail it is possible to find out who is working on what module and when they started and/or finished.

ArchiveWork

The *ArchiveWork=<path> configuration parameter* specifies that PVCS is to work on a copy of an archive file rather than on the archive file directly. If ArchiveWork is in effect, then a copy of the archive file is copied into the directory specified by <path>. If, for any reason the machine goes down during a PVCS operation, perhaps because of a power failure, only the temporary copy will be effected. The worst case scenario would be to have a power failure during the time that PVCS is copying the temporary archive file copy over the actual archive file. When the power fails, the archive file is corrupt because the copy did not finish. In this case, the system administrator needs to copy the temporary file over the corrupted archive file to recover because the temporary copy is the complete archive file. If NoArchiveWork is in effect, then a power failure may cause corruption of the archive file that is not recoverable.

An additional consideration for the ArchiveWork=<path> configuration parameter is the <path> component. If the archive files are stored on a file server, then the ath component should indicate a directory that is on the server. If the <path> is a workstation directory, network loading will increase and performance will decrease as data is transferred across the network.

Network-specific configuration parameters

There are five network specific configuration parameters, *Semaphore, SemaphoreDir, SemSuffix, SemaphoreDelay* and *SemaphoreRetry*. The first is "Semaphore [archive location] = [semaphore type]." This configuration parameter tells PVCS commands to use semaphores to coordinate multiple accesses to a single archive file. The [archive location] specifies where the archive files reside, either locally on the workstation or on the network file server. The [semaphore type] component specifies the type of semaphore to use. These may be "NetWare" for Novell NetWare API calls, "OS/2" for OS/2 where a single user may be able to access the same file through multiple sessions. The "OS/2" specification should not be used if the OS/2 machine is connected to a network in which archive files are stored on the server. The third specification for [semaphore type] is "file," which can be used in all other circumstances where semaphore use is advised.

The SemaphoreDir=<path> configuration parameter specifies the directory in which semaphore files will be maintained. It is recommended that regardless of whether or not SemaphoreDir is used, it should be disallowed to ensure that all semaphore files are created and maintained in the same directory. Semaphore files in different directories are worse than useless as the purpose of the semaphore is defeated.

SemSuffix=<suffix template> allows the default file suffix for semaphore files to be renamed. Of much more pragmatic use are the two remaining network-specific configuration parameters. SemaphoreDelay=<n> where <n> is in tenths of a second specifies how long a PVCS command that fails due to the presence of a semaphore should wait before retrying to access the archive file. By default, each PVCS command will wait 2 seconds (SemaphoreDelay=20) before trying again to complete the command.

The final network specific configuration parameter is Semaphore-Retry=<n> where <n> specifies the number of times to try a command before reporting a failure. The default setting, (SemaphoreRetry=3), is to try the command three times before termination.

Enforcing policy

There are a number of decisions to be made prior to establishing a Master Configuration File. However, once those decisions are made, they should be adhered to by all users. To accomplish this, any and all configuration parameters that indicate policy should be disallowed. Regardless of how strictly policy is to be enforced, some configuration parameters should be disallowed to insure the integrity of the security system and of the archive files. At a minimum, AccessDB, Login and CheckLock should be disallowed. Fig. 10.8 illustrates some recommendations that might be appropriate in almost any work environment. The optional disallowed parameters should be used as appropriate, depending upon the environment. For example, if VCSDir is set in the Master Configuration File, then it may well be that it is not desirable for users to alter its setting. In this case, VCSDir should be disallowed.

Flexibility in all things

There are many configuration parameters that have not been discussed. Many of them target the individual user and allow the user to establish a working environment that suits his or her own tastes. For example, the VCSEdit configuration parameter allows a user to specify

Recommended Usage

```
DISALLOW ACCESSDB AUTOCREATE  CHECKLOCK EXCLUSIVELOCK
DISALLOW FIRSTMATCH JOURNAL LOGIN LOGWORK SEMAPHORE
DISALLOW SEMAPHOREDIR MULTILOCK
```

Optional Usage depending upon Environment

```
DISALLOW WORKDIR VCSID VCSDIR
```

Figure 10.8   Enforcing policy.

an editor to be called up automatically whenever a description, either workfile or change, is requested by the PVCS "PUT" command. In general, any configuration parameter that will not affect security, archive integrity, or system performance should not be disallowed so that individual users may create their own PVCS environment in which to work.

The Local Configuration File

Individual tastes are best expressed in a local configuration file. A local configuration file is read by PVCS independently from the Master Configuration File as described. A local configuration file is a configuration file that exists in the working directory. Because it is local to a specific directory on a specific machine, any settings established in a local configuration file are not reflected back into the system operation definition. For this reason, it is best for personal choices to be reflected in a local configuration file.

Multiple Configuration Files for Multiple Tasks

One very powerful aspect of the local configuration file paradigm is that by changing the working directory, the user can change the setting of configuration parameters. For example, if a user is working on more than one set of source files at any given time, that user can create several working directories to match the different sets of source files. Refer to Fig. 10.9. In each working directory, a local configuration file could set VCSDir to a different archive directory than the VCSDir specified by a local configuration file in another working directory. By changing working directories, the user changes the setting of VCSDir. This prevents confusion as the user cannot check a workfile into the wrong archive should the workfile have the same name as another workfile from a different project. Using individual settings for VCSDir also enhances system performance as directory searches can be restricted to only the archive directories relevant to the working directory. Because PVCS is no longer searching all archive directories, the archive search is completed in less time.

At a higher level, the same concept can be carried out in the Master Configuration File. As discussed previously, a unique setting for the VCSDir configuration parameter can be obtained by using an environmental variable, such as PROJECT. However, the use of environmental variables to define access to directories that may or may not be sensitive is asking for trouble. Anyone can set an environmental

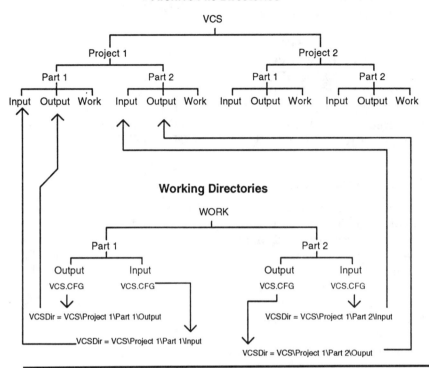

Figure 10.9   Local configuration files limit archive searches.

variable to anything. Sure, access control security may prevent the legal access to those archive files, but hackers are hackers, and no security system is completely invulnerable. If a person sets their environmental variable to an "illegal" definition and then invokes a PVCS command, the command will fail but the user will learn the name of the archive directory.

Perhaps a better way to parse VCSDir definitions is to do so by user name in the Master Configuration File and then disallow VCSDir. The drawback to this method is that the Master Configuration File must be edited each time a new user is added, a user moves from one project to another, or any other personnel change occurs. The first advantage is that the VCSDir mapping cannot be defeated. Another advantage is that users are mapped to precisely the archive directories desired.

Because the VCSDir setting can be made to be cumulative, special users can be mapped to multiple VCSDir settings. To make VCSDir setting cumulative, the directory listing must begin with a semicolon. The VCSDir setting can also define a root archive directory. Defining a root archive directory causes PVCS first to search the root archive directory and then all archive subdirectories beneath the root. Root directories are specified by using an asterisk, "*", as the last element in the directory specification.

Refer to Fig. 10.10. PVCS will only search the archive directory "H:\VCS\PROJECT1\INPUT if the user is "mikes". PVCS will search both "H:\VCS\PROJECT1\INPUT" and "H:\VCS\PROJECT1\OUTPUT" if the user is "peter". Finally, if the user is "joer", PVCS will search the archive directory "H:\VCS\PROJECT1" and all archive subdirectories directly beneath "H:\VCS\PROJECT1".

Reference Directories

A reference directory is a directory in which browse copies of modules are kept for project tasks. For example, source code would be kept in a reference directory for compilation purposes. The advantage of a reference directory is that any user who requires access to modules for any non-editing purpose may access the latest revisions of the modules without checking out the modules. Less time is required as the PVCS programs do not have to be invoked to obtain copies of the modules. Software builds are assured of using the latest and greatest of all modules automatically.

A single reference directory for each project could easily be defined by using the configuration parameter "ReferenceDir = [directory]". The directory can be absolute, for example "H:\VCS\PROJECT1\REFERENCE",

Excerpt from Master Confguration File

```
%if  "$(VCSID)" == "peter" || "$(VCSID)" == "fredm"
        VCSDir=;H:\VCS\PROJECT1\PART1\INPUT
%end .


%if  "$(VCSID)" == "peter" || "$(VCSID)" == "mikes"
        VCSDir=;H:\VCS\PROJECT1\PART1\OUTPUT
%end

%if  "$(VCSID)" == "joer"
        VCSDir=;H:\VCS\PROJECT1\*
%end

DISALLOW VCSDir
```

Figure 10.10   Use of cumulative and global VCSDIR specifications

or the reference directory can be relative to the archive directory. For example, if the archive directory is "H:\VCS\PROJECT1\PART1\ INPUT" and the reference directory definition is "ReferenceDir = *\..\ REFERENCE", then the reference directory is "H:\VCS\PROJECT1\ PART1\INPUT\REFERENCE".

Mapping the project hierarchy

There are two ways in which the projects archive directory hierarchy can be mapped to reference directories. To obtain an exact mapping of where all subdirectories of both the archive and reference root directories are named identically, the configuration parameters VCSDir and ReferenceDir are used. Each of these configuration parameters should specify a root directory. For example, "VCSDir = H:\VCS*" and "ReferenceDir = H:\REF".

To create a unique mapping of reference directories to archive directories, use only the VCSDir configuration parameter. In the VCSDir specification, name the reference directory for each archive directory by placing the reference directory name in parentheses immediately after the archive directory name. Figure 10.11 illustrates a unique reference directory mapping. By defining reference directories in this manner, multiple archive directories can be mapped to a single reference directory while other archive directories are mapped to their own reference directory.

Specialized Tasks

There are a number of specialized tasks that PVCS is very good at. If disk space is at a premium, then archive file compression can be employed at very little performance cost for a large storage gain. If a remote site or the mainframe requires update, delta records, which specify changes from one revision to the next, can be transmitted, saving time and transmission costs. Promotion groups can be defined wherein project tracking is constrained to a limited set of life-cycle stages.

Configuring for compression

There are three configuration parameters that are used to specify archive file compression. *The configuration parameter CompressDelta* is used to specify that only delta records are to be compressed. The latest revision (the tip) is kept in standard format. The *configuration parameter CompressWorkImage* is used to tell PVCS to compress the latest, (and since it is whole, largest), revision only. Finally, the *configuration parameter compress* specifies that PVCS is to compress the entire archive file, thereby gaining the smallest archive file possible.

Configuring for updates

A *delta file* is a file that specifies how a revision of a module must be changed in order to become another revision, (hopefully newer). If a remote site uses source modules, then the developing agency can transmit to the remote site delta files that specify the changes to make to the current modules in order to bring them into alignment with the newest revisions. Likewise, source developed on a local area network that will run on a mainframe can be uploaded using the same delta file paradigm. Instead of uploading a complete new source listing, the smaller delta files can be uploaded and the source on the mainframe updated.

There are four configuration parameters that help to define the contents and command structure of delta files, *Delta Delete, Delta Insert, Delta Replace*, and *Delta Seq*. "Delta Delete = 'format string'" specifies the delete line command for the updating process. "Delta

Excerpt from Master Configuration File

VCSDir = H:\VCS\PROJECT1\PART1\INPUT (H:\SRC\P1P1)

VCSDir = ;H:\VCS\PROJECT1\PART1\OUTPUT (H:\SRC\P1P1)

VCSDir = ;H:\VCS\PROJECT1\PART1\WORK (H:\SRC\P1P1)

VCSDir = ;H:\VCS\PROJECT1\PART2\INPUT (H:\SRC\P1P2\INPUT)

VCSDir = ;H:\VCS\PROJECT1\PART2\OUTPUT (H:\SRC\P1P2\OUTPUT) .

VCSDir = ;H:\VCS\PROJECT1\PART2\WORK (H:\SRC\P1P2\WORK)

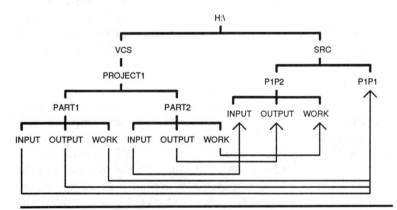

Figure 10.11   Archive and reference directory specification.

Insert = 'format string'" specifies the insert line command. "Delta Replace = 'format string'" specifies the replace line command. COBOL programmers can make use of the 'Delta Seq = "<start>-<end>"' configuration parameter to specify column sequence numbers. PVCS provides a special code for columns 1 through 6, "Delta Seq = COBOL."

Configuring promotion groups

Promotion groups are used to control and track software (or other project types) through the life cycle. After deciding on and defining promotion groups as applicable to an organization, the promotion groups are readily implemented into PVCS with the "Promote" configuration parameter. Use the "Promote" configuration parameter as illustrated in Fig. 10.12 which illustrates the hierarchy of some sample promotion groups and how those groups are defined in the Master Configuration File. Note that the definitions define a hierarchy implicitly.

Hierarchy of Promotion Groups

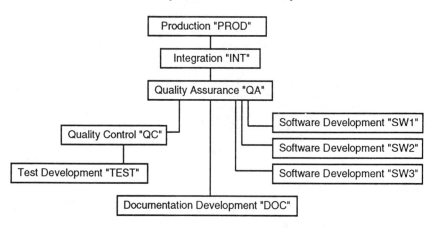

Excerpt from Master Configuration File

Promote Doc QA
Promote SW1 QA
Promote SW2 QA
Promote SW3 QA
Promote TEST QC
Promote QC QA
Promote QA INT
Promote INT PROD

Figure 10.12   Configuring for promotion groups.

Summary

Setting up and configuring PVCS is not a difficult task but neither is it trivial. Many decisions must be made before the configuration can start. Will a Master Configuration File be used? Will enhanced access security be used? How will the user identification be obtained?

Once installed and configured, PVCS is very flexible. Individual users can customize the actions of PVCS to their own taste through the use of a local configuration file.

Questions

1. Under what circumstances should a user's ability to specify a VCSDir through their own local configuration file be curtailed? Name at least three.

2. If a user has a local RAM disk on their workstation, would using the local RAM disk be better than using a file server's standard disk drive for the ArchiveWork directory. Why or why not?

11

Automation of
Project Tasks

One of the benefits of the information age is the accuracy that can be applied to tasks formerly performed by human beings. If a machine is properly programmed to perform a given task, that machine can complete the task far faster than any human, and with a fair certainty of accuracy. As intelligent as the human species is, it is still prone to making errors.

As the complexity of a task grows, so also grows the potential for human error when performing that task. A very simple task, such as adding two integers may be performed within a few seconds with a very good chance that the answer is correct. If the task is complicated in some fashion, such as adding a thousand integers, not only does it take the human a significant amount of time to complete the task, the chances that the result is accurate are greatly diminished, regardless of the intelligence or aptitude of the human performing the task.

In comparison, a small and rather primitive computer can perform the same two-integer addition in a few milliseconds with one hundred percent accuracy. A personal computer can add several thousand integer numbers in just a few milliseconds, again, with one hundred percent accuracy. A parallel processing super computer can add several million integer numbers in just a few milliseconds, yet again with one hundred percent accuracy.

Adding numbers is a simple task. Compiling a single source module is a simple task. Deriving a model for ocean current interaction is a very complex task. Coordinating the accurate compilation of the correct source module revisions and linking them into an application program is also a complex task. Fortunately, the computer performs the compilation and the linking so that those tasks are relatively easy to accomplish. Unfortunately, the computer must be told exactly how to compile each module and what modules to link in what order.

Imagine a software system composed of several hundred source modules. Each module must be compiled with the exact same compiler invoked with the exact same parameters. How many humans would be absolutely confident that they had made no errors, specified no extra parameters, or forgotten any required parameters, in invoking the compiler several hundred times in a row? Even if the human is completely self-assured about the compiler invocations, can the human be as confident that the correct revision of each module was compiled? After six months go by, can that human be sure that they can rebuild the system exactly the same as it was done originally?

If you could find a person who had such ability and confidence, and the confidence was based upon fact rather than ego, that person would be in possession of talents worth millions to many computer software manufacturing firms. But no such human exists. No matter how smart or experienced we are, we still make mistakes.

Fortunately, we humans are aware of our weaknesses and have invented tools that compensate for our inabilities. One such tool, invented over twenty years ago, is the *make* program.

The Make Program

The first make programs are still in use today. They were simple programs that read a file, called a makefile, that contained a listing of the ingredients of a program and a listing of how they were to be constructed and combined. Each module required to build the system has its own construction definition. A target, that which is being constructed, is listed along with components, called dependencies, which are required to construct the target in one line of the makefile. The next line of the makefile contains the instructions (commands) required to produce the target from the dependencies.

A makefile for a large project may consist of thousands of lines of targets, dependencies, and instructions. Such a makefile requires construction and maintenance, which may prove to be a full time task. Even with make, there is no way to guarantee that the correct revisions of the components were used to produce the target.

Make, the Next Generation

In the late nineteen eighties, the make program began to evolve thanks to a relatively small company based in the Pacific Northwest, Polytron

Incorporated. The company became quite successful by producing UNIX tools for the DOS and OS/2 environments and by taking those tools and improving them. The original Source Code Control System (SCCS) had not changed in nearly twenty years. Its successor, the Revision Control System (RCS) was a big improvement, but still left much to be desired. The third generation of source code control system was a vast improvement. The first two generations have not changed since they were originally authored. The third generation, the Polytron Version Control System, while no longer a product of the now defunct Polytron Incorporated, is constantly evolving.

Source code control was not the only new generation product produced by the wizards at Polytron. The original make was redesigned with a different design paradigm: rule-based decision making. In addition, the new make, originally called "PolyMake" and now called the "PVCS Configuration Builder," was integrated with the PVCS version control product, and for the first time a make program could be used that ensured that the correct revisions of the component modules were used to construct the target. Since the time that Polytron came out with PolyMake, several other software tool companies have revised their make utility products to emulate the rule-based power of PolyMake. Today, there are several products from several major manufacturers that emulate some of the features of PolyMake. However, PolyMake, like PVCS Version Manager, continues to evolve and the competitive products lag several years behind in make technology. PolyMake is now known to the marketplace as the "PVCS Configuration Builder" and is marketed by INTERSOLV, the same good folks that market PVCS, now known as the "PVCS Version Manager." The makefile for the PVCS Configuration Builder has been renamed to "build script" to differentiate it from earlier make products.

Rule-Based Decision Making

The application of rule-based make utilities is quite simple when compared to the older direction-oriented make programs. The benefits of using a rule-based make utility are many. Rule-based build scripts are much smaller and far easier to maintain. To illustrate this fact, consider a simple program's construction under both forms of make utility.

Figure 11.1 shows a makefile used to construct a simple ".COM" program to run under DOS. The first target to be constructed is the source module, which depends upon an archive file. Note that this simple target is limited in that a separate makefile would be required to construct any revision of the module other than the first. The next

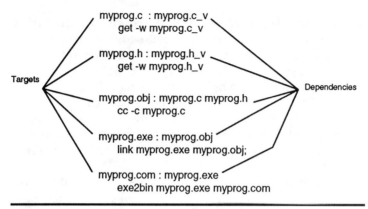

Figure 11.1   Simple makefile for standard make utility.

target to be constructed by the makefile is the object file, which is produced by compiling the source and include files. The third target is the executable program whose dependency is the object file. The fourth target is the ".COM" file.

Note that no decisions are made by the make utility interpreting the makefile in Fig. 11.1. Each step is explicitly spelled out. Only one computer language is specified and only one set of basic components is used.

Figure 11.2 illustrates some generalized rules used in rule-based make utilities. The PVCS Configuration Builder comes out of the box with a set of default rules already defined. The user may redefine those predefined rules and may also create brand new rules as desired.

```
.c_v.c :
    get $(_GetOpts) $(_SourceRev) $(_Source) $(_Target)

.c.obj :
    $(CC) $(CFLAGS) -c -Fo$(_Target) $(_Source)

.asm.obj :
    $(AS) $(AFLAGS) $(_Source) $(_Target):

.obj.exe :
    link $(LFLAGS) <@<
$[Separators"+ \n", $(_Sources)]
$(_TargRoot)
<

.exe.com :
    exe2bin $(_Source) $(_Target)
```

Figure 11.2   Samples of generalizes rules.

To define a rule, the file suffix (extension) of the source module is listed after a period. A second period separates the source file suffix from the target file suffix. On the very next line, the command line to be used to produce the target from the first is listed. There need be nothing mysterious about the command line as it specifies a command exactly as it would be entered if done by hand. The rules in Fig. 11.2 appear a little mysterious in that they make use of some other powerful features of the product, context and system macros.

Figure 11.3 compares a standard makefile with a build script for the PVCS Configuration Builder. The final target, a ".COM" program constructed from a single-source module for both the makefile and the build script, is identical.

Figure 11.4 illustrates the decision path used by the rule-based PVCS Configuration Builder to construct the ".COM" program whose build script is illustrated in Fig. 11.3. Bear in mind while comparing the makefile and the build script that the decision tree that the make program constructed is very primitive and the simple executable is based on one and only one source module. If the complexity for the standard make is four or five times that of the rule-based build script for a single module, imagine the difference between the makefile and the build script for a very large and complex program.

Controlling the Development Environment

When a large software project is constructed, it is the combination of the efforts of a team of people that are combined. It is very important that each and every member of the team construct their portion of the

Standard Make	Rule Based Make
utility.c : utility.c_v get -w utility.c	target : utility.com
utility.obj : utility.c cc -c -Foutility.obj utility.c	
utility.exe : utility.obj link utility.exe utility.obj;	
utility.com : utility.exe exe2com utility.exe utility.com	

Figure 11.3 Makefile comparison.

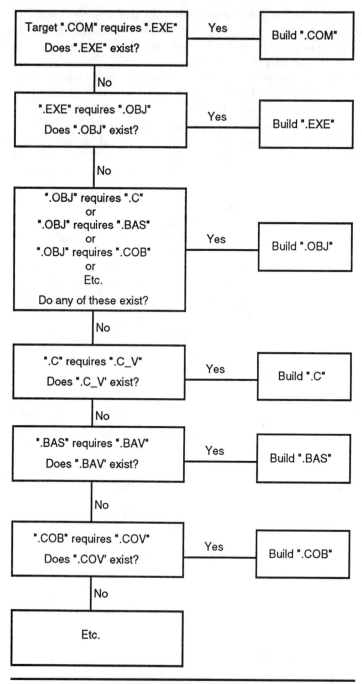

Figure 11.4   Decision flow chart for simple ".COM" program—rule based make utility.

project in exactly the same fashion and manner as every other team member. It could prove to be a big problem if, for example, half of the team compiled modules using the small model with near pointer calls while the other half of the team used the large model with far pointer calls. The resultant program may or may not work. If the program was carefully designed to use mixed-model programming, the team may have a chance at succeeding. If the design assumed the same model throughout, the team will be very lucky indeed if the program does not crash the first time it is run.

Commonalty of construction rules can be obtained very easily with the PVCS Configuration Builder. The PVCS Configuration Builder looks for rule files in almost the exact same manner as PVCS Version Manager looks for configuration files. When the PVCS Configuration Builder is invoked, it first looks in the local directory for a file named "BUILTINS". If it finds the file, it reads it and uses the rules defined therein. If it cannot find the "BUILTINS" file, it next looks in the local directory for "BUILTINS.MAK". If "BUILTINS.MAK" is not found, the PVCS Configuration Builder then looks for an environmental variable "BUILTINS". If the environmental variable "BUILTINS" has been defined, the definition represents the name of a global rule definitions file, PVCS Configuration Builder will read the file so defined for its rule definitions.

The user can optionally specify a different rule file from the command line, and in the absence of any such rule file, PVCS Configuration Builder will use rules that are predefined and embedded into the PVCS Configuration Builder by default. In the future, INTERSOLV plans to move away from using individual rule files and toward a centralized initialization file, normally called "tools.ini".

Maintaining separation of new and old

Perhaps the most critical issue in the software development environment is ensuring that the most recent revisions of source code modules are used during software builds. Even if the build target is meant only to test and debug one small subsystem, it is important to ensure that the "latest, greatest" revisions are used. The accuracy of tests and the validity of debug information depend upon inclusion of the latest, and hopefully, best revisions of all modules.

There are a number of ways to accomplish the goal of using only the latest revisions in the build process. The simplest solution is to use the PVCS Configuration Builder with its built-in rules concerning archive files. Extensions to those rules are easily accomplished in the global rules file or in the individual make files. The drawback to this approach is that for each and every module to be compiled, time must be taken by the PVCS Configuration Builder to check out the latest revision of each module. While the time taken may not be excessive in a small build environment, as the number of modules increases, so does the time to check out the latest revisions.

The reference directory

A less time consuming method of obtaining the latest revision of all modules is to reference a reference directory's path in the build script. By using the ".Path" directive, as illustrated in Fig. 11.5, the PVCS Configuration Builder will look in the directories specified when a source file is not located in the current working directory. The same directive can then be used in specification of dependencies. Recall that a dependency is an ingredient necessary to construct the target. Using the ".Path" directive to specify both the reference directory and the archive file directory in the build script specification will cause the PVCS Configuration Builder to test the target's status, that is whether or not it is up to date, against the actual ingredients used in the target's construction. In the example, if a source module in the reference directory were out of date, (this should never happen, but it never hurts to take out some insurance), it would be immediately updated.

Figure 11.6 illustrates a segment of another build script. In this example, all object files are defined under one macro definition. For legibility, sets of object files in given subsystems are defined in groups. The final overall object file specification macro is the collection of all other object file naming macros. A multiple-path ".PATH" directive is used to specify the reference directories for the system components. Finally, a pseudo target name is used to specify the ultimate target and

```
#    Building the graphical user interface sub-system

#    The .Path.C directive specifies the reference directory
#    The .Path.C_V directive specifies where the archive files
#      for the modules can be found, if needed.

.Path.C=C:\USR\REFERENCE\SRC\PROJECT\GUI;
.Path.C_V=C:\USR\VCS\PROJECT\GUI

#    Re-define default generalized rule to assure latest trunk revision.
.c_v.c:
      get -w $(.Path.C_V)$(_Source)($(.Path.C)$(_Target))

# Build Script continues from here.
```

Figure 11.5   A segment of a subsystem build script.

```
GROBJS=  <list of object file names> \
         <list of object file names> \
         <list of object file names>
MENUOBJS = <list of object file names> \
           <list of object file names>

PROJOBJS = $(GROBJS) $(MENUOBJS)

.Path.C=C:\USR\SRC\PROJECT\GUI; \
        C:\USR\SRC\PROJECT\STATES; \
        C:\USR\SRC\PROJECT\ENGINES; \
        C:\USR\SRC\PROJECT\FUNCTIONS; \
        C:\USR\SRC\PROJECT\DATA; \
        H:\SRC\GRAPHICS\COMMON; \
        H:\SRC\PROJECT\COMMON

.Path.C_V=C:\USR\V CS\PROJECT\GUI; \
        C:\USR\VCS\PROJECT\STATES; \
        C:\USR\VCS\PROJECT\ENGINES; \
        C:\USR\VCS\PROJECT\FUNCTIONS; \
        C:\USR\VCS\PROJECT\DATA; \
        H:\VCS\GRAPHICS\COMMON; \
        H:\VCS\PROJECT\COMMON
```

```
MENUSYS : $(PROJECT).exe

$(PROJECT).exe : $(PROJOBJS)
```

Internal Rules Used
.c_.v.c:
.c.obj :
.obj.exe :

Figure 11.6   **A build script using built-in generalized rules.**

the ultimate target is defined as depending on all of the object files. The pseudo target is complete when the single component it consists of is complete. No further definitions are necessary as the built-in rules can accomplish all required tasks without further guidance.

The project hierarchy

However you architect the hierarchy of your project, it is the correct way for you to do so as long as it makes sense to you. There are no wrong ways, only better ways. It is usually recommended that the project hierarchy be implemented through a directory tree with related functionality incorporated into a branch of the directory tree. For example, if a subsystem of the project is a graphical user interface, (GUI), then all code related to the GUI should fall under a directory whose name signifies the GUI. Subdirectories of the "GUI" directory may be "mouseio", "keyboardio", "menusys", or the like. The hierarchy of the version-control directories may be mirrored by reference directories as discussed above. The version control directory hierarchy can also be mirrored in whole or in part by an individual's working directories. Refer to Fig. 11.7. The VCS and Reference directories reside on the file server. An individual who works on the GUI subsystem may have a set of working directories as illustrated.

Automation in Revision Management

More often than not, an engineering change, a bug fix, or whatever task is the task of the moment, will result in changes in more than one module. Most times, the modules altered are interrelated and are all edited and altered between updates to the version control files. If the only files residing in the working directories are those files that were edited, then managing the check-in of the new revisions of these modules is a simple thing. However, the engineer or programmer may not have foreknowledge about which modules will require changes. In this case, the individual may elect to check out for edit all modules that may require modification. Whether or not the module really needs to be edited cannot be determined until the editing process is complete. In this case, it is possible that the developer may or may not remember which modules were changed and which were not. Regardless, the changed modules must be checked in.

In this case, a good practice is to attempt to check in all modules using the "-n" option, which tells PVCS not to abort the check-in process if a module is discovered with no changes. Figure 11.8 illustrates a DOS batch file "CHECKIN.BAT" which loads check-in batch files and programs into a RAM disk for performance sake. "CHECKIN.BAT" then calls "PUTEM.BAT" which changes working directories so that the local "VCS.CFG" files can be used. "PUTEM.BAT" is listed in Fig. 11.9. "PUTEM.BAT" constructs a "message" that will be used for the change description and then calls "UPDATE.BAT," which is listed in Fig. 11.10, for each file of the specified suffix in the directory. "UPDATE.BAT" then attempts to check-in a new revision. If it fails, it will attempt to create a new archive file. If it succeeds, it will check in the initial revision. If it fails, it means that the archive file already exists and that the module was not altered.

Note that the three batch files check to see if a message has been entered by the user. No check-in will be performed unless a change message is entered. The disadvantage with this method is that all archive files will receive the exact same change description. Worse yet is the fact that any newly created archive files will have the change description for their module description.

A revised set of batch files is illustrated in Figs. 11.11, 11.12 and 11.13. The batch files are simpler in that they do not have comment

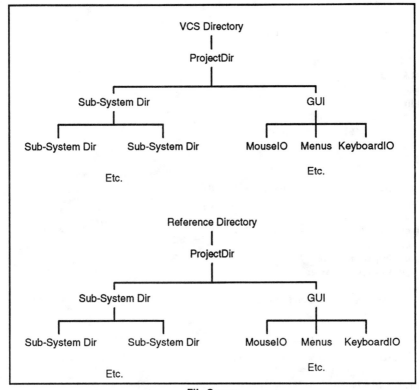

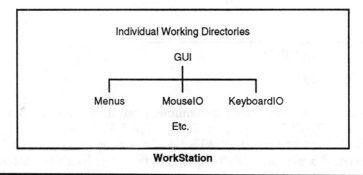

Figure 11.7

```
@echo off
rem
rem First verify comments entered
rem
if "%1"=="" goto doit
set Message=%1
:loop
shift
if "%1"=="" goto doit
set Message=%Message% %1
goto loop
:doit
rem
rem    Setup, copy executables to the ram disk.
rem
cp c:\etc\putem.bat e:
cp c:\etc\update.bat e:
cp c:\bin\pvcs\rse.exe e:
cp c:\bin\pvcs\put.exe e:
cp c:\bin\pvcs\vcs.exe e:
rem
rem Change drives and go to work
rem
E:
echo Begin processing source files
call putem %Message%
c:
rm e:\putem.bat
rm e:\update.bat
rm e:\rse.exe
rm e:\put.exe
rm e:\vcs.exe
exit
```

Figure 11.8   CHECKIN.BAT.

collecting loops. Other than the comment building loop, the first two batch files, "CHECKIN.BAT" and "PUTEM.BAT" are essentially the same as before. The file "UPDATE.BAT" has been greatly revised and enhanced. If a module revision check-in fails, the batch file attempts to create a new archive file. If the archive file already exists, the VCS program returns an error code, which means that there was no change to the module. If the archive file does not yet exist, it is created and the user asked to enter a module description automatically by the VCS program. If a new archive file is created, the first revision is checked into the archive file.

```
@echo off
if "%1"=="" goto nomess
set Message=%1
:loop
shift
if "%1"=="" goto doit
set Message=%Message% %1
goto loop
:doit
c:
cd \usr\design\fastd
echo Checking in BUILD and COMMAND files
for %%f in (*.mak *.bat *.cmd) do call e:\update %%f %Message%
cd src
echo Checking in source files
for %%f in (*.c *.for *.asm *.cob) do call e:\update %%f %Message%
cd ..\include
echo Checking-in include files
for %%f in (*.h *.inc) do call e:\update %%f %Message%
cd ..
echo Checking-in complete
goto done
:nomess
echo Usage:
echo    checkin Your Comments
echo    (Used only for checkin of design/fastd)
echo    ......................................
echo    Example:  checkin A test of the new stuff
:done
```

Figure 11.9.   PUTEM.BAT.

Both sets of batch files use the "-l" option to the PUT command. This option causes PVCS to immediately check out the new revision with a lock for edit. If continuing edits of the modules are not a concern, then remove the "-l" option from the command lines contained within the batch files.

Automation in the Build Process

As discussed in the previous chapter, the build process can be a very complex operation. If accomplished by hand, the process may involve executing hundred of commands. The more complex the operation, the more room for human error. The PVCS Configuration Builder as well as all other make utilities automate this process. If the makefile or build script is constructed correctly, then human error is eliminated.

```
@echo off
set File=%1
set Message=%2
:loop
shift
if "%2"=="" goto doit
set Message=%Message% %2
goto loop
:doit
e:\rse e:\put -n -l -m"%Message%" %File% > nul
if errorlevel == 1 goto nofile
Echo New revision for %File%
goto done
:nofile
rem
rem %File% is either non-existent, or more likely, has no new revision
rem
rem vcs -i -n %File%
rem Enforces file description entry.
rem
rem vcs -i -n -t"%Message%" %File%
rem  Uses comment as workfile description
rem
e:\rse e:\vcs -i -n -t"%Message%" %File% > nul
rem
rem Now, if there was no change, we are finished
rem
if errorlevel == 1 goto done
rem
rem However, if no error, then we created an archive
rem file, check in the new revision
rem and notify the user.
rem
Echo New file %File%, archive file Created
e:\rse e:\put -l %File% > nul
:done
```

Figure 11.10   UPDATE.BAT.

There are also some distinct benefits when automating the build process. Let us examine some of these benefits.

Build minimization

If the build process is conducted by hand, then the operator must perform a significant evaluation of the states of all components or, to ensure that no errors occur, build the entire system every time a build is required, for

```
@echo off
rem Setup, copy executables to the ram disk.
rem
cp c:\etc\putem.bat e:
cp c:\etc\update.bat e:
cp c:\bin\pvcs\rse.exe e:
cp c:\bin\pvcs\put.exe e:
cp c:\bin\pvcs\vcs.exe e:
rem
e:
echo Begin processing source files
rem
call putem %Message%
c:
rm e:\putem.bat
rm e:\update.bat
rm e:\rse.exe
rm e:\put.exe
rm e:\vcs.exe
exit
```

Figure 11.11   Revised CHECKIN.BAT.

any reason whatsoever. The operator must ensure that no object file is younger than any one of its dependencies. If the average source module depends upon five include files and there are hundreds of source modules, then the operator must check at least five hundred dependencies.

A make program checks these dependencies automatically and constructs only those components that are out of date. Because the process

```
@echo off
c:
cd \usr\design\fastd
echo Checking in BUILD and COMMAND files
for %%f in (*.mak *.bat *.cmd) do call e:\update %%f %Message%
cd src
echo Checking in source files
for %%f in (*.c *.for *.asm *.cob) do call e:\update %%f %Message%
cd ..\include
echo Checking-in include files
for %%f in (*.h *.inc) do call e:\update %%f %Message%
cd ..
echo Checkin-in complete
```

Figure 11.12   Revised PUTEM.BAT.

```
@echo off
set File=%1
rem
rem Read comments from the comment file that is
rem associated with the module through the
rem MessageSuffix directive
rem
e:\rse put -n -l -m@ %File% > nul
rem
rem If an error, the check to see if archive file exists
rem
if errorlevel == 1 goto nofile
Echo New revision for %File%
goto done
:nofile
rem
rem %File% is either non-existent, or has no new revision
rem Use VCS -N option to halt archive file overwrite
rem automatically
rem
rem vcs -i -n %File%
rem
rem Ask the user for a description of the workfile
rem (a default operation)
rem vcs -i -n %File% will as for the description.
rem
e:\rse vcs -i -n %File% > nul
rem
rem Now, if there was no change, we are finished
rem
if errorlevel == 1 goto done
rem
rem However, if no error, then we have created an archive
rem file, notify user
rem
Echo New file %File%, Archive file Created
rem
rem And perform the check-in.
rem
e:\rse put -l %File% > nul
:done
```

Figure 11.13   Revised UPDATE.BAT.

is automated, the user need only invoke the make program and relax as the make program constructs the target application.

Often times a developer will be the only developer of an application or subsystem thereof. When this is the case, the developer usually finds that he or she is the only person editing a given set of files. In this case, the developer may wish to keep a working copy of each module in his or her working directory. Each working copy has a revision locked in the archive file. During the development process, the developer needs to check the altered modules into their respective archive files while retaining the locked revisions of the files that have not been altered. Assuming the developer is using the "C" programming language, this periodic check in can be accomplished with the command line:

PUT -L -N *.C *.H

Naturally, the above command can be modified for any type of computer language. The "-L" option tells PVCS to immediately check out a new revision with a lock. The "-N" option tells PVCS to ignore unchanged files and keep working.

There is one drawback to the above system. The newly checked-in files are recompiled immediately upon a build command whether or not they really need it. Checking in an "include" file in this manner will cause all modules to be recompiled. The solution to this drawback is the "TOUCH" command. The "TOUCH" command updates the time and date of the specified files to the current time and date. If the existing state of all modules is such that the last build operation was successful, then no module really need recompilation. To prevent the unnecessary recompilation, use the following command line:

PUT -L -N *.C *.H;TOUCH *.OBJ

This command can be issued as two separate commands if desired. Because the "TOUCH" command is run after the check-in process, all object module files have a more recent time and date stamp than the source and include files. There is a danger in this method. If an include file is changed, the change requires recompilation of the modules, and all the modules are "touched," then the modules that need to be recompiled will not be and the system may experience catastrophic failure.

Rule-based construction

Until recently, all make utilities, with the exception of the PVCS Configuration Builder, required explicit rules for all components. A typical make file for an application constructed from less than one hundred source modules could be as long as two thousand lines. For the most part, this is still true today.

The PVCS Configuration Builder has several additional rule types as well as a collection of macro types, loop types, conditional constructs, and functions that make construction of a makefile or build script much simpler and easier to manage. The makefile that was two thousand lines long can be converted to a build script of less than one hundred lines.

Adding intelligence to the build process

A PVCS Configuration Builder build script can invoke any process or application that a human computer operator can. Where a user would have to check the DOS "errorlevel" to determine a success or failure, the build script can do the same using the "%Status" built-in function. For example, a build script can be used to automatically check in any changed module by using a conditional construct with the %Status built-in function. To do so, the "VDIFF" program with the "-t" option can be run on the source module which compares it to the archived latest revision. Figure 11.14 illustrates an explicit rule with a decision construct and the same rule rewritten as a generalized rule. If %Status evaluates to a zero, then the files are identical. If %Status evaluates to a one, then an error of some kind has occurred. If %Status evaluates to a two, then the files are different and the new revision should be checked in. A conditional construct that evaluates the value of %Status can then make an "intelligent" decision regarding the situation and act accordingly. In the example, the decisions are to abort the operation after displaying an error message or to check in a new revision if the files are different. Whether the files are different or the same, if no error occurs in the "VDIFF" process, the file will be compiled.

Time-saving techniques

When constructing a small project, the time it takes to do so may not seem significant. However, when the project begins to grow and exceeds perhaps 20 modules, the issue of performance becomes very real indeed. There are several techniques that can be used to speed up the performance of the PVCS tool set.

One of the greatest improvements in speed can be realized if a RAM disk is used for temporary files and for memory swapping. The PVCS Configuration Builder checks for an environmental variable "TMPSWAP" to determine in which directory to perform memory swaps of program memory to free as much conventional memory as

Explicit Rule

```
Example.OBJ: Example.c
      vdiff -t example.c example.c_v
      %if %Status == 2
            put -u example.c
            %if %Status == 1
                  %echo ERROR checking in Example.c
                  %Abort
            %endif
      %endif
      #
      cl /AL /Foexample.obj example.c
```

Generalized Rule

```
.c.obj:
      #
      # Test the source against the archive
      #
      vdiff -t $(_Source) $[Base,$(_Source)].??v
      #
      # If they differ, check in the new revision
      #
      %if %Status == 2
            put -u $(_Source)($[Base,$(_Source)].??v)
            #
            # If the put fails, notify and abort.
            #
            %if %Status == 1
                  %echo ERROR checking in $(_Source)
                  %Abort
            %endif
      $endif
      #
      $(CC) $(CFLAGS) -c -Fo$(_Target) $(_Source)
```

Figure 11.14   Decision-making constructs.

possible for invoked applications. The PVCS Configuration Builder looks for an environmental variable "TEMP", "TMP", or "WORK" to determine the directory in which to place temporary working files and data. The PVCS Version Manager looks for a directive "WorkDir" to determine in which directory to place temporary working files and data. For optimum performance, set "TMPSWAP", "TEMP", and "WorkDir" to indicate a RAM disk directory. The PVCS Version Manager has another directive, "ArchiveWork", which tells the Version Manager where to place temporary copies of archive files. This directory should never be a RAM disk for security reasons as the file would be lost forever if a power failure occurred. User's of older versions of the PVCS Version Manager will recognize the "ArchiveWork" directive as "LogWork". It has the exact same definition as "ArchiveWork" and is maintained for backwards compatibility.

Automated notification

Some events are such that other personnel should be notified when they occur. Other events should cause reports to be generated so that the user can be more effective in his or her job. For example, if a change is made in a requirements or specifications document, those persons who are responsible for implementing the requirements or designing to the specifications should be notified immediately. In another example, a modified source code module needs to be tested against all other modules that call on, or are called by, the modified module.

Because a build script can invoke anything that a human can invoke, the build script can be used to invoke an electronic mail message should a change be made in a type of document. In our first example, a specification modification is made. Although not usually included in a makefile or build script, specifications and requirements documents can be addressed by the build script. A rule can be constructed that invokes an electronic mail program and delivers a message to a given list of persons should a change in one of the specifications or requirements documents occur.

In a second example, a source module is modified. If the modification was the addition of a new calling parameter, then any and all other modules that call the modified module must themselves be modified. If the change is not so drastic, it is still a good idea to verify that no other module is adversely affected by the modification. When the software system is constructed, the build script can be constructed so that an impact analysis is generated for each changed module, as shown in Fig. 11.15. The result is that the user automatically receives a listing of all modules that may be affected by the change. It may be that the user does not want to be notified of such possible impacts until he or she is certain that the modifications are complete. In this case, an alias may be defined at the command line that specifies that the notification is to occur using the operating system "set" command to establish an environmental variable.

Note: At the time of this writing, PVCS does not provide an impact analysis tool. It is expected that INTERSOLV will provide such a tool in the future as an impact analysis tool is a very important piece of the configuration management pie. When and if this occurs, please refer to your PVCS Version Manager documentation for the correct calling name and parameters and replace the "vimpact" command in the figure with the correct command.

Application of the Build Process

To most software engineers and to almost every support person, the build process is limited to constructing the software system and no

Command Lines:

```
> Set NOTIFY=ON
> Make Target
> Set NOTIFY=
```

Build Script Generalized Rule

```
.c.obj:
     #
     # Test source file against the archive
     #
     vdiff -t $(_Source) $[Base,$(_Source)].??v
     #
     # If they differ....
     #
     %if %Status == 2
          #
          # Check in the new revision...
          #
          put -u $(_Source)($[Base,$(_Source)].??v)
          #
          # If the put fails for any reason
          # notify and abort.
          #
          %if %Status == 1
               %echo ERROR checking in $(_Source)
               %echo Aborting Build procedure...
               %Abort
          #
          # If it works, test for potential impact
          #
          %elseif $Defined(NOTIFY)
               vimpact$(_Source) > $[Base,$(_Source)].imp
               %if %Status == 1
                    %echo ERROR Impact Analysis Error
                    %echo Source file: $(_Source).
                    %echo Notify system administrator.
               %Abort
          %endif
     $endif
     #
     $(CC) $(CFLAGS) -c -Fo$(_Target) $(_Source)
```

Figure 11.15 Automating impact analysis notification.

more. However, this is far from the truth. A build script can be constructed to perform any and all repetitive tasks. If there is a given procedure that is repeated on a regular basis, that procedure is a candidate for a build script. If a formatted report is due every Friday afternoon, and the contents of the report differ only in content that is generated by an information retrieval system, then the construction of that report would be faster and more accurate if put under control of a build script. In actuality, many tasks that have little or no relation to the software construction process can be automated by using a build script.

Documentation

Assume that there is a base product that is sold in many different system configurations, a computer motherboard for example. The documentation for the sold configurations is identical, with the exception of the chapters that describe the various options to the system as configured. Assume further that the chapters for the various options are kept in separate files. By placing the documentation construction task under the control of the PVCS Configuration Builder, the author may construct an exact and correct manual by specifying the target configuration when invoking the "build script." A difficult and error prone task has been automated.

Quality assurance and control

Quality assurance and control groups can also benefit from implementation of the PVCS Configuration Builder. Test script invocation can be automated such that many tests can be conducted sequentially with no human interaction. The PVCS Configuration Builder will normally stop after an error has occurred, but by using the ".KeepWorking" directive, even if an error occurs, the remaining tests will be conducted. In this fashion, all tests can be run during a single session. Results can be echoed to the screen or written into a result file for later examination.

Testing and development tools

Testing tools, just like compilers and linkers or even source codes, are constantly being upgraded and altered. These tools, programs and scripts should be maintained under version control. When a test needs to be repeated for any release of a product, the exact same tools that were used originally can be invoked again by the PVCS Configuration Builder if the build script is constructed to do so.

If it is necessary to reconstruct a given software system, it is very important that the exact same tools used in the first place are used for reconstruction. If an old release of a product suffering from a bug that must be duplicated and fixed is still in the field, it would not do to reconstruct it with newer releases of compilers and linkers because the executable image would not be the same as the original. It would be impossible to perform a meaningful debug session under these conditions. What if the bug were caused by an optimization performed by the compiler and that bug was fixed in the new release of that compiler? The bug would disappear, surely. But you would not know the reason that the bug disappeared. What if the bug disappeared because of a new bug in the new release compiler that, by chance, countered the effect of the bug in the code? Is it a good idea to introduce unknown factors into a problem that requires solution? Of course not. How do you prevent this from happening?

The best solution to this problem is to keep copies of all revisions of all tools used. For example, if you use a C compiler, the compiler must reside somewhere on disk for it to be used. Instead of storing the compiler in a directory, say "E:\tools\compilers\c", add another level of directories and store by revision. You would store revision 5.5 of the C compiler in the directory "E:\tools\compilers\c\r5.5" and revision 6.0 of the C compiler in the directory "E"'\tools\compilers\c\r6.0". Now, when you construct the build script for the product, include the compiler path, either explicitly or by macro definition under the target's revision or version name. If, at some future time, the revision or version must be reconstructed, the correct tools will be invoked automatically.

Release management

Each release of a software system should be identified by a version label. When a new release is made, each component revision should be assigned the release level identifying version label. Figure 11.16 illustrates a generalized rule that tests to see if the macro "VERSION" has been defined. If so, it checks out the required revision associated with the defined "VERSION" and uses it for compilation. If "VERSION" is not defined, it examines the source module in the local directory and compares it to the latest revision in the archive file. If they are different, it checks in the new revision prior to compiling it. The "-u" option tells the PVCS Version Manager to retain a copy of the workfile in the local directory but to remove the lock after checking in the new revision. If continued work is expected on the module, the "-u" option can be changed to "-l" so that the archive file remains locked with the user's identification and continued editing can occur.

Summary

Every repetitive task can be automated with a little thought and a build script. From program or document construction to weekly report generation, automation greatly simplifies the task and reduces the human error factor to near zero. The only remaining chance for errors is in the user's construction of the build script.

Many of the features of the PVCS Configuration Builder have not been discussed. These include some of the various types of macros that can be defined under the PVCS Configuration Builder. These macros are extremely powerful. It is recommended that you study them in detail and learn how to use them.

```
.c.obj:
        #
        # If a version is defined, then build the version.
        # To do this, check out the appropriate revisions
        #
        %if %Defined(VERSION)
                get -w -q -v$(VERSION) $(_Source)($[Base,$(_Source)].??v
        #
        # If no version defined, we are building with code that may
        # be new, This build script attempts to force a checkin.  If
        # it fails, it aborts after printing an error message.
        #
        %else
                #
                # Test for differences
                #
                vdiff -t $(_Source) $[Base,$(_Source)].??v
                #
                # If the file differs from the archive file's
                # latest revision, attempt to check in.
                #
                %if %Status == 2
                        put -u $(_Source)($[Base,$(_Source)].??v)
                        #
                        # If the put fails, (user does not have lock),
                        # tell the user about the failure but do not abort.
                        #
                        %if %Status == 1
                                %echo Error checking in $(_Source)
                        %endif
                #
                # If a problem in the test occurs, then tell the
                # user about it and abort.
                #
                %elseif %Status == 1
                        %echo ERROR: Testing archive for $(_Source)
                        %echo Aborting Build procedure....
                        %Abort
                        %endif
                %endif
        $endif
        #
        $(CC) $(CFLAGS) -c -Fo$(_Target) $(_Source)
```

Figure 11.16   **Version extracting generalized rule.**

Questions

1. Many compilers come with their own make program. Why replace the free make program with the PVCS Configuration Builder?

2. Describe how to construct an old version of a product using the free make program and compare the makefile for the process with a similar build script.

3. Is there a way to make a makefile recognize version labels? How or why not?

12

Information Retrieval

One of the most important aspects of a configuration management system is its ability to provide specific information in response to a wide variety of information requests. The information provided is in itself a valuable tool in managing and developing a software system. For managers and project leaders, configuration management provides the ability to monitor the progress of all or part of the development project and to monitor the progress of team members. Managers can also use the information to produce and update accurate work schedules and to provide interactive load-balancing among the team members.

Managers are not the only team members to benefit from the ability of a configuration management system to provide project information. Developers can make use of the information as a debugging aid, as a revision history monitor, and as a development tool. Maintenance engineers can make use of the information to determine the exact contents and revision levels thereof used in the construction of various product releases. Testing engineers can use the information to determine alterations to modules since the last test cycle. The list of developer uses goes on and on.

The information provided by a configuration management system is invaluable and flexible. The user can extract precise information that will enable them to better perform their assigned tasks and help them to maintain development schedules.

The Management Perspective

The needs of management are basically twofold in nature. Project leaders and managers need to be able to determine the state of the development project in order to intelligently discuss issues and schedules. Personnel managers need to be able to track the production, problems, performance, and workload of individual team members. While many developers will not initially appreciate the performance-tracking aspect, they are almost certain to alter their negative view when they consider the benefits. Performance tracking allows a manager to perform work load-balancing. Performance tracking also gives a manager the ability to locate the laggard and take appropriate action. Developers, in all honesty, should not object to this (unless of course they are the laggard!). Everyone wants everyone else to pull their fair share of the workload too!

The project state

There are many aspects of the project state. The project state could represent the percentage of completed and debugged modules. It could represent the revision levels of all modules. The project state could represent the modules or subsystem currently under development as compared to the system as a whole. The meaning of the term *project state* is variable as well. What the project state means to one person at one level may be entirely different than what it means to another person at another level. Regardless of the meaning or interpretation of the name, a good configuration management system should be able to provide the information requested, whatever it is, to indicate the project state. The nature of the information may change to satisfy the user's definition of *project state*, the ability to produce the information should be virtualized, that is, it should not care what the information is. This means that the configuration management system must be prepared to answer a lot of different requests. To be prepared, the archive files must be complete and must store all significant information about the represented file and its history of changes. That is why so much information is stored in the PVCS Version Manager archive file.

Assume for a moment that the project state for one individual is represented by the revision levels of the state's component modules. A report that specifies the latest revision level of each module can be generated by issuing the PVCS Version Manager command:

```
VLOG -BN *.??V.
```

This command generates a report consisting of one line for each module in which the module name is printed along with the number of the latest trunk revision for that module. A manager may peruse this report and find that most modules have a similar revision range, for example from 1.4 to 1.8. Any module that has a much higher revision level may need some special consideration. It is obvious by the high number of revisions that something is wrong. Perhaps the code is suffering repeated revamping to get it to work. Maybe the specification was too broad and the code body quite large. Maybe there is no way around a complex piece of code. Perhaps the system design needs reevaluation. Perhaps, if only one person is working on the module, that person does not fully understand the purpose of the module, or how it should perform its tasks. Maybe there is a fundamental conceptual problem. Whatever the reason, the fact that only one or two modules have a very high revision level indicates that something needs investigation. Our manager got enough information out of one simple command to know that he or she should find out more information and perhaps prevent a calamity.

If the current revision report needs to be generated for a custom release or a port of the application to an alternate platform whose revisions are managed on archive file branches, the user merely specifies the branch as follows:

VLOG -BN<*branch_number*> *.??V

Naturally, most branches related to a given project will not have the same level. The code in module A was ready at revision level 1.4, therefore, its branch number is 1.4.1.x where module B was not ready until revision level 1.6, giving its branch number as 1.6.1.x. The disparity in branch number is not an abnormal occurrence, in fact, most related branches will have different numbers. To keep from having to issue the VLOG command many times with various branch numbers and modules specified, and to keep from having to track which module has which branch number, the "DefaultVersion" directive can be used to specify a version label associated with each module regardless of the branch number. If the version label *Windows Version* is attached to each of the branches in each of the modules, then by defining the DefaultVersion directive in a configuration file, a single command is all that is necessary to generate the branch report. Because PVCS Version Manager will use the version label defined by DefaultVersion by default, the command to produce the report becomes simply:

VLOG -BN *.??V

The command is exactly the same as the one used to generate the latest trunk revision report. The difference is the use of the DefaultVersion directive in a configuration file.

Now, let us assume that the project state is represented by the percentage of modules that have been promoted from the development promotion group. To determine which modules have been promoted and are ready for testing, the manager could issue the command:

VLOG -BG*test_group* *.??V

This command generates a report that shows which revisions of each module, if any, have been promoted to the "test_group" promotion group.

If a manager or other user wishes to determine which modules are currently under work-in-progress, he or she can issue the command:

VLOG -BL *.??V

This command generates a report that specifies and lists the revisions of the modules that are currently locked, regardless of who has locked them.

If a manager or other person wishes to find out the revision levels of the modules associated with a given release, identified by a version label, or perhaps a version of interest, he or she may issue the command:

VLOG -BV*version_label* *.??V

This command generates a brief report that specifies all the modules that contain the version label and what revision that label is associated with. This can be especially handy for customer support personnel who need to determine if a given module has changed, and if so, how it has changed since the version that the customer is complaining about was made.

Who is doing what to which?

The VLOG command is very powerful in that it provides a wealth of information. Not only can it be used to determine the project state, but the workload and performance of individuals.

Assume that every Friday afternoon, a given manager generates a report using the following command to determine what revisions are locked and who has them out for edit:

VLOG -BL *.??V

Our manager notices that one of his employees has had one, and only one, module locked for the last three weeks. The revision levels have changed, but work is still in progress. Our manager can then speak to the employee to determine if there is a problem. Is the design faulty? Does the employee understand the task? Help can be brought to bear, obstacles overcome, and progress made, but only if the problem can be identified in the first place.

From the same report, our manager notices that another of the employees seems to have many locked modules that are constantly rotating. During the first week the employee had seven modules locked. The next week, the same employee had nine modules locked, but only two of them were the same as the week before. Is the employee trying to solve everyone else's problems? Is the employee overworked? Why so many modules? Why the constant shift? Is there really a problem here? Whether or not a problem exists, the manager is alerted to the potential of a problem and can investigate. The manager can then communicate, analyze, and perhaps solve or avoid a problem completely.

Another manager wishes to determine which modules are currently under work by three members of his or her development team. What is that portion of the team working on now? To find out, the user names can be specified in the command line as follows:

VLOG -BL*john,linda,sue* *.??v

This command generates a brief report that lists the module names and revisions locked by John, Linda and Sue. There are many more options to the VLOG command that allow it to produce a variety of reports. What is important is what is done with the information. The information can be used constructively or counterproductively. The PVCS Version Manager can provide the information, it cannot control the morality or ethics of the user. The information can be used to balance work loads and identify problem areas, and it can be used to tightly monitor the production and work quality of individuals. Such information can be used to further the goals of the team, identify and correct team weaknesses and problems, and enable the development environment.

The Integration Perspective

There are several aspects of integration engineering. One such aspect is the integration of the subsystems into the system as a whole. Another aspect of integration engineering is the relation and compatibility of the developed system with other systems, either internally generated or purchased.

It is entirely possible for each of many subsystems to completely conform to their individual specifications, pass all testing requirements, and still not work together when combined. One or more subsystems will typically fail when many are integrated into a whole system. As development continues, the list of failed subsystems may shrink, expand, and perhaps rotate among the member subsystems.

Each iteration of a tested subsystem should be identified with a version label. Assume that subsystem A integrates with no problems and is identified as such with a version label. If, at some future time, subsystem A fails the integration tests, the exact changes between the current version and the successful version can be easily determined and the reason for failure found much more rapidly then by a system of trial and error debugging. A detailed report can be generated by entering the system working directory to obtain the correct configuration information and then issuing the command:

VDIFF -V*good_version* -V*new_verion* *.??V

Naturally, this concept can be expanded to include the entire system when testing against integration with other software systems.

Release Engineering's Perspective

A release engineer is responsible for ensuring that the correct revisions of all concerned components are used in the construction of a given release. Under older revision tracking tools, this entailed generating a report of the revision levels for each module and the revision levels of all the tools used to produce the release. The problem is that the report must be maintained somewhere and must be kept somewhere safe. The loss of such data would be a catastrophe.

Fortunately, the PVCS Version Manager provides version labels to completely eliminate this task. When a release is made, it is identified by a version label that is assigned to the correct revision of each module used in constructing the release. It is the version label that eases the tasks associated with release management as well as reduces the stress associated with maintaining hard or soft copy records used to track revision levels in one form or another.

Members of a version

All too frequently, a release engineer is asked to find out which revision of a module was incorporated into a given release. Development or maintenance engineering needs to verify a bug, or enhance the code, or some other task that requires the exact revision from some given module. If our release engineer has access to the PVCS Version Manager, his or her job becomes very simple. A single command will generate the required information. In this case, the command would be:

VLOG -BV*version_label module_name*

To find the revision levels associated with the entire release:

VLOG -BV*version_label* *.??V

Tool identification

Another item of extreme importance is tracking the revision levels of the tools used to produce the system. Tools change as upgrades are released and bugs fixed. One revision of a given compiler may optimize code in a completely different manner than the next release of the compiler. Perhaps some anomaly in the source code allows the code to compile under one release of the compiler but not another. Perhaps the software system is constructed such that the method of optimization is known and "dirty" shortcuts are integrated into the code to take advantage of or work around compiler features.

Regardless of why, because there are a million different reasons, it is a good idea to track the tool revisions as well as the module revisions. Perhaps the easiest way is to maintain all revisions of all tools in some fashion and reference that maintenance in the project build script.

In Fig. 12.1, the tools directory is used to maintain all revisions of all tools that were or are used to construct a product release. As long as the product release is on the market or in use by customers, the directories in which the tools used to construct those releases are

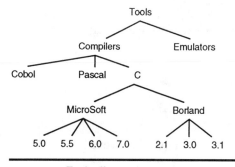

Figure 12.1   Tools directories.

maintained. Once no product release uses a specific version of a given tool, the associated tool subdirectory can be deleted.

In Fig. 12.2, a build script, the tool directories are referenced in the build script so that any time a release needs to be reconstructed, the correct tools are invoked. The build script is maintained under PVCS Version Manager control so that it may continue to grow and be modified to match the current release level. Each revision of the build script is stored with a version label that identifies the release with which it is associated.

In order to construct a release with the exact tools used when the release was originally made, the user retrieves the build script revision with the same version label as the release to be reconstructed. The user then can invoke "BUILD" to use that build script and have absolute faith that the release will be reconstructed exactly.

The custom release

A custom release is a special version of the software system produced for a special customer, purpose, or function. Like any other release, a custom release needs to be reproducible. Fortunately, the PVCS Version Manager version label can be constructed using any legal ASCII characters and can be up to 254 bytes long. If the version label will contain spaces, tabs, or asterisks, then it must be enclosed in quotation marks. This means that the version label can say anything that you want it to. A custom release to Fred Jones and Daughter, Inc. may be identified with a version label "The custom release for Fred Jones and Daughter, Inc. made on Jan. 28, 1993 because we like Fred." Of course,

```
Use Macros to Define the Tools



     Revision 1.3 of the "build script"
           version label "BETA"

CC = DevSys:\Tools\Compilers\MicroSoft\5.0\CL.EXE




     Revision 1.5 of the "build script"
         version label "Release 1.0"

CC = DevSys:\Tools\Compilers\MicroSoft\6.0\CL.EXE
```

Figure 12.2 Tools revision tracking through build scripts.

using such a version label would be silly. In the first place, a PVCS Version Manager user would have to enter the version label exactly as specified, which would mean a lot of typing with a great potential for error. A better version label would be "Fred Jones and Daughter R1.0," or perhaps "Jones 1.0." Even if the user forgets the exact version label used, or did not know it in the first place, a report can be generated that specifies all version labels so that the user can obtain any version label desired. The command to generate such a report is:

VLOG -BV *.??v

Because no specific version label is identified on the command line, the report will list all version labels associated with all modules.

The current release

When assigning a version label to the current release, one common mistake is to assign the version label to the latest trunk revision with one sweeping command:

VCS -Vversion_label *.??v

The problem with this approach is that, all too often, one or more modules has been modified after promotion to the test promotion group and the latest trunk revision represents work in progress for the next release. If configuration management techniques have been employed, the revisions associated with the new release already have a version label assigned, most likely something to do with testing. For our purposes here, assume that the version label "TESTOK" was used to identify those revisions that passed testing and are part of the new release. In this case, we would want to replace the "TESTOK" version label with a version label that identifies the release level of the product. Let us define that version label as "RELEASE 1.2". The command to accomplish the upgrading of the version label and identify the release would be:

VCS -V"RELEASE 1.2"::TESTOK *.??v

Past releases

If configuration management is relatively new to the organization and past releases were not stored under the PVCS Version Manager, it is not very difficult to implement release management under PVCS Version Manager for those releases. If revision management was maintained by another product, for example SCCS, then the process is even easier. PVCS Version Manager provides some utilities to convert archive files from another system, like SCCS, into PVCS archive files. If the tool in use in the past does not have a converter, then the job is a whole lot harder because you must extract one revision at a time and check it into PVCS to construct the archive files with full history.

The next step is to identify the past releases. To do so, you must know the revision level of each module that was associated with each past release. Once this information is obtained, the process, while tedious, is relatively easy. For each module, you assign the correct version label to the correct revision for each release. The command to associate a version label with a particular revision is:

VCS -V*version_label:revision module_name*

While this may seem a tedious task that is a waste of time, the very first time that an older release must be constructed, the time and effort will be repaid.

Current work

The last thing a release engineer or manager wants to do is to include current work revisions into a release. Each module in a release must have been tested and verified. If integration is a concern, then the integration engineers must verify the integrity of the system. To include current work may be a fatal error in terms of the software systems viability. For this reason, it is absolutely imperative that release revisions be identified with a version label. Not only that, but the build script must reference the version label so that the correct revisions are used regardless of whether the person who invokes the build remembers to specify the correct version label. Finally, when the build occurs, insurance must be taken that no current work object files are linked into the system by mistake. Either the build must occur in an object file free directory or the build must be invoked with the "ALL" flag. Using the "ALL" flag ensures that all modules will be re-compiled regardless of the presence of newer object files that may or may not represent current work.

The development version

There are times when the development version of the software system is to be released to a limited set of customers. These releases are often called *alpha* or *beta* releases. Because the code is in a constant state of flux, it is extremely important to identify the module revisions associated with such a release.

The first time a product is released in prerelease condition, that is an alpha or beta release, identification is simple. However, when the first official release has been made and the second release is under development, the problem of how to identify individual beta releases arises. Perhaps the user finds out about the problem when they try to assign the beta version label and PVCS Version Manager asks them if they are sure that they want to delete the old beta version label. Perhaps they are aware that the warning message will come and prepare for it. How do they prepare? The first thing to do is to pick a new name for the first beta release. Perhaps "BETA 1.0" for the beta release for official release 1.0 and "BETA 1.1" for release 1.1, and so on. Next, rename the old beta release to "BETA 1.0", then assign the new beta or "BETA 1.1" to the new beta release revisions. Here are the commands to do so:

VCS -V"*BETA 1.0"::BETA* *.??V

VCS -V"*BETA 1.1"* *.??V

The second command assumes that the new beta release consists of the latest revisions from the trunks of the archive files. If this is not the case, adjust the command accordingly by adding the appropriate version label.

The test version

More often than not, it is a test version that becomes a release version. Perhaps the test version goes through several steps prior to release. Each test phase can be identified by a version label. For example, when a system is first promoted by engineering it may become the *"FUNCTIONAL TEST"* version. When it passes functional test, it becomes the *"INTER-FACE TEST"* version. When it passes interface testing, it may become the *"INTEGRATION TEST"* version. When integration testing is complete and the system passes all tests, it may then be considered for a release. Perhaps it is then identified as the *"TESTED_OK"* version.

No matter how the test version is identified, all revisions of all modules in the new release must have successfully passed through the test cycle before promotion to the release version can occur. No exception should be made except under the most extreme emergency conditions. Using the "TESTED_OK" version label to identify those module revisions that successfully passed all tests is a good way to identify valid revisions.

Building the new release

Once all revisions of all modules associated with a software system have passed their exams, then they are ready to become members of the new release. One of the modules that passed its tests should be the project build script. The release engineer assigns a version label to all appropriate revisions including the build script revision. It is up to the release engineer to verify the build script references, precise tool revisions, and the correct release version labels.

Once the build script version labels have been verified, the release engineer should insure that the build script that he or she just modified does, in fact, build the system as specified.

The Developer's Perspective

The developer of software systems has a unique and intimate relationship with the interrelated modules that are used to produce the system. The developer eats, breathes, and dreams about the code. Nobody knows the internal workings of the system better than the implementing engineers and programmers.

Yet even with this intimate knowledge, the software developer has a set of oft-occurring problems. No matter how intimate the knowledge of the system, some problems are very difficult to solve. It is these problems, the illusive or intermittent new bug and the reintroduced bug, that can cause irreparable delays in the development schedule. Imagine a software system constructed from over one thousand modules. A programmer solves one problem with one of the modules and rebuilds the system. When the system is tested, it demonstrates a new software "feature" that is not desirable. Naturally, the programmer would suspect the module that he or she just altered. Tracking down and repairing the problem should be easy.

Now, imagine that there are 20 programmers involved in the project. The system as constructed so far works on Friday, but on the following Thursday the new software system crashes. Now, whose work should be checked? Even if every programmer checks their work for the past five days and all programmers report that their code is good, the system still crashes. Why? Perhaps because a change made by one programmer is interacting with a change made by another programmer.

Determining the nature of such a bug is a very difficult job indeed. Even with a good debugger, the search may take a very long time, days, maybe weeks, sometimes even months.

Tracking down the new bug

There is no excuse for a prolonged bug search if configuration management tools have been put in place and configuration management techniques are employed. Finding the new bug should only take a matter of minutes. In the worst case, perhaps a few hours. How can configuration management reduce the search time?

If a journal, otherwise known as an audit trail, file has been specified in one of the PVCS Version Manager configuration files, then the job becomes quite simple. Assume that the last working version of the system was constructed with code dated October 5, 1992. It is now October 8, 1992. The first thing to do is to determine the names of all modules that have changes since the system last worked. To accomplish this task, issue the command:

VJOURNAL -D*Oct 5, 92** -O*PUT journal_file_name.*

The above command tells PVCS Version Manager to generate a report listing each module that was checked in (PUT) on or after October 5, 1992.

The next step is to evaluate the report. If some idea exists of where the problem lies, then the report may give a good indication of exactly where to look. If no such idea exists, then evaluation of the report still will give a good idea of where to look! The report will also tell you where you do not have to look.

The next step is to generate change reports for all suspected modules. If there is a chance that the error is caused by a modification in a module, it is worth the small effort required to generate a change report if for no other reason than to eliminate the module from the search.

To generate the change report for each changed module, first determine the revision numbers of the superseded revisions. To do so, use the VLOG command:

VLOG -BR -D*Oct 5, 92* *.??V

This command generates a brief report that specifies the revisions current on the specified date, in this case, October 5, 1992. This report will be used to generate an exact difference report for each module. To generate the difference report, issue the command:

VDIFF -R*old_rev* -R *archive_file_name.*

This command generates a report comparing the old revision specified in "old_rev" against the latest revision in the archive file specified by "archive_file_name." The latest revision is referenced by default because the second "-R" option does not specify a revision number.

The complete difference report should give every indication of the problem or its nature. The exact changes are readily visible and how those changes interact can be determined by analysis. However, a very difficult software "feature" may require even further investigation. Perhaps one of the changes to one of the modules affects a module that was not changed in some adverse manner. In this case, a where used document should be generated, and impact analysis should be performed.

An impact-analysis-generated where used document will list all modules that call on or invoke the specified module. As of this writing, the impact analysis report producing programs from InterSolv are still on the drawing board, so an example of how to use the command is not feasible. However, later in this book a method for producing this type of report is discussed in the section on building the missing tools.

The reintroduced bug

One problem faced by developers is the reintroduced bug. Fortunately, it is not encountered very frequently. Unfortunately, it is a serious problem when it occurs. If configuration management techniques and tools are in place, then the problem should become extremely rare. Even rarefied, the problem can be a difficult one to solve.

Perhaps the build script that was used to construct the system is in error and references an older revision. This would seem to be the most likely cause for a bug that has already been repaired to surface anew. Another possible cause might be that the wrong revision of the module was assigned the version label associated with the current system build. However, if promotion techniques are used, this is extremely unlikely.

Current work load

There are a number of problems that arise during the software development process that are immediate in the perspective of the software developer.

Often, changes made to a module will not work as expected. If the changes are fatal or, if the developer suddenly discovers a better way to accomplish the goals, a recovery of the last state of the module is quite easy as long as configuration management techniques have been followed. In this case, the developer can restore the module to its prior state by issuing the command:

GET -W -Y *module_name*

This command will overwrite the working copy of the module with the latest revision checked into the trunk of the archive file. The above command should be modified if the developer is working on a branch, that is unless, of course, the developer has set the DefaultVersion directive in a configuration file.

The importance of comments

Source code should be well commented. A fairly good rule of thumb for a minimal comment content is one line of comments for every two lines of code. Source code comments are particularly useful when making a bug fix. The original code should be commented out, but retained as a comment. The reason for the change should be commented as well as the thinking behind the change.

Source code comments are not the only comments that belong with a module. When the module is first designed, it has a specific purpose. That purpose should be documented in the module description requested by PVCS Version Manager when the archive file is first created. From then on, each new revision will receive a change description. As has already been discussed, it is not sufficient to input, "Fixed a bug," or "Added some functionality," or some other equally brief statement. The change description should give a brief description of what was changed, how it was changed, and why it was changed. The change description can be brief as long as it is complete.

If the change description is complete, then a developer tracking down a newly introduced bug can view the change descriptions and make decisions about which modules require the complete change listing with much better accuracy. The change description does not have to be a mirror of the comments concerning change in the code that are in the code itself, but should give an indication of the actual changes.

Application of the changes made

Often times, the development team for a given project is really a composition of several teams, sometimes from different locations. If those locations are not connected via network, then application of changes to modules can be a time-consuming process. There are several ways to address the problem of updating remote code sites.

If one development team resides in one building, or on one floor, and another development team resides in another building or floor, then one way for one team to update the other is by *floppy net*. That is, a team member creates one or more floppy disks with the updated source and hand carries it over to the other team. This method, while far from automated, has worked well for many years providing that great care is taken in the manufacturing of the diskettes. The floppy net solution will not work if the two teams are separated by more than just a few hundred yards.

If the development teams are separated by a distance that is not easily walked, then the problem may be saved by modem communications. The new source code is transmitted over the modem to the other site. The drawback to this solution is that if there is a significant body of code to transmit, the modem process is both time-consuming and expensive. There is a better way to accomplish the task.

The PVCS Version Manager command "VDIFF" provides a mechanism by which a *delta script* can be created. A delta script is similar in content to the report generated by the "VDIFF" command when the user is searching out exact changes to a module. The sending site creates a delta script for each module that the remote site needs to have updated. The delta scripts are then transmitted over the modem. Because the delta scripts are much, much smaller than the full source code, the transmission time is greatly reduced as is the telephone expense. The remote site can then run the PVCS "REGEN" command to upgrade their modules to the current revision level.

To generate the delta script, the user must know the revision levels of all the modules at the remote site. Hopefully, they are identified with a version label. For example purposes, assume that a version label is used and call it the *"remote_revision"* version. The user must also be able to identify the upgrade revisions. The command:

VDIFF -D -V*remote_revision* -R *module_name*

compares the older *"remote_revision"* with the latest revision on the trunk. The command should be modified as necessary to compare exact revisions if the remote site is not to be updated to the latest trunk revision. Usually, the remote site will receive revisions that have already been tested. In this case, the command would be:

VDIFF -V*remote_revision* -V*tested_version_label module_name*

Updating the host

Those developers who are producing code that will eventually run on a mainframe computer need to be able to update the version control systems located on the mainframe whenever a new production release of the system is made. The mechanics for doing so are almost exactly the same as for updating a remote site. Fortunately, the PVCS Version Manager has provided several command-line options to the "VDIFF" command that cause it to produce delta scripts that target several popular mainframe version control products. In addition, an automated update transmission program is available in the PVCS Production GateWay product.

Summary

Regardless of the perspective under which a software system is evaluated, configuration management tools should be able to provide information that is relevant to the perspective. In other words, the configuration management tool set should be able to answer almost any question it is asked. The ability to do so provides a very powerful tool and aid to the software development process.

Questions

1. Generating reports with a configuration management tool like the PVCS tool set is easy. How would you find the difference between two revisions of a file without the aid of a configuration management tool set?

2. How would you generate a report that specifies the modules currently under development? Could you? What difficulties and obstacles must be overcome to do so?

3. How would you generate a report that specifies the names of the modules that one person is working on and how long they have been working on them? Could you? How could you verify your findings? Could you? Why or why not?

13

Source Code Interrelationships

The Cross-Reference

One very important tool that is almost indispensable in a large scale development environment is the cross-reference. There are two basic types of cross-references. The first is a cross-reference that can be used to determine all the modules that call on a specified function or procedure. This cross-reference is commonly called the *where used document*. The second type of cross-reference is used to determine which modules would be affected if a change in a data structure were made. This type of cross-reference is called the *data impact statement*. The *where used document* and the data impact statement are produced by a process commonly called *impact analysis*.

Impact analysis

The first cross-reference, the where used document produced by impact analysis, is the most frequently used and is an invaluable tool. A developer may find that he or she uses the impact analysis tool on a very regular and frequent basis. Its strength lies in the fact that it can tell a developer the names of all modules that must be evaluated or modified because the programmers have modified a module. Assume that a programmer modifies a module to such an extent that failure to modify any other module that references the modified module will cause catastrophic system failure. What kind of change could have such a drastic effect? Usually it is something very simple. Maybe a new parameter is added to the function definition, or the definition, and therefore return value, of the module is altered. A function that returned an integer now returns an unsigned long integer. When the program is tested, good data turns into garbage. A passed array is now half the size it used to be and the receiving function violates memory by trying to write into some other data object's memory space. If it succeeds, good data turns into trash. If it doesn't then the user eventually finds that he or she is staring at an error message that is soon followed by an operating system prompt. "The application has violated application memory space, please quit all applications and reboot." is a message that no developer likes to see. Where did it happen? In what code? How can it be found and fixed quickly?

For example, if a module is modified such that it now has a different number of calling parameters, then all modules that reference or invoke the changed module must be modified. The programmer must often determine the names of all of the modules that reference a modified module in order to be able to modify them as well. The programmer must find each reference to the changed module in each of the listed modules and add the new parameter or change the received data's definition. Without an impact analysis tool, the developer must do a manual search through all source code modules looking for references to the modified module. A manual search can be accomplished by changing the working directory to the reference directory or directories (if they exist) or to whatever directory the source code is in, and using a tool such as "FGREP" to locate references. ("FGREP" is a file searching program with pattern matching capability). However, while it may seem a straightforward process, the manual process is tedious and error prone. The user must change directories into each of the source directories, run the text-search program, and make hand-written notes of his or her findings. This solution relies on the premise that all such source directories are accessible by the user, that the user knows the names of all such directories, and that the user takes perfect notes.

A much better solution is use of an automated tool. Some programming environments now come with primitive tools that produce limited information. Within a subsystem they are of some use. The problem with such a system is that each time any module is compiled, an additional process occurs to produce a record that is stored in its own file. When the target of the build process is constructed, the master database file is updated. Much productive time is wasted on trivial changes that do not have any effect on the database. The impact upon performance is such that only when a bug is the result of a code change and the bug cannot be found by any other possible means, will the programmer set the cross-reference option in the environment that creates the database.

Data impact statements

Data impact statements are similar to the where-used document in that the report lists a number of module names that may be impacted by an action. A data impact statement is useful when a data structure requires modification. Each and every module that references the modified data type must be examined to determine coding modification requirements.

For example, say an application program lets you reduce a text "window" to an icon. The icon is specified in a data structure that specifies the upper left-hand corner of the icon. It is exactly 100 pixels by 100 pixels in size (a picture element on a display screen). The location of the icon is stored in a two-element integer array, the first element representing the horizontal screen coordinate and the second representing the vertical screen coordinate for the upper left-hand corner of the icon. The requirement for the next release of the application specifies that the icon be dynamically resized by the user. In order to accomplish the requirement, the data structure that represents an icon must be redefined. The integer array is expanded to contain four integers, thus specifying the upper left-hand and lower right-hand corners of the icon's screen location. If all icons are drawn, moved, resized, and erased from a single module, then there is no real problem. The one module is modified and the work is done. However, it is much more likely that several, if not all, of the icon-related functions reside in different modules. Each one of these modules must be updated to make use of the new location specification.

The above example is rather simple in that only a few modules may be affected by a data structure redefinition. In a large scale application, where many modules make use of a given data type, the process of identifying those modules becomes complex. This is especially true when the application consists of more than one subsystem and the source code for each resides in a different directory.

Implementing a Cross-Reference

Hopefully, the PVCS tool set will soon be augmented by the introduction of an impact analysis tool to generate where used documents. If you do not yet have access to an impact analysis tool and need to produce one, or if you already have one but wish to understand how they work, this section of the chapter may be of special interest to you.

If you are going to produce a cross-reference tool, you must first pick a tool to build it with. A cross-reference generator can be produced using almost any computer programming language. However, just because it can be produced doesn't mean that it is easy to produce.

Some computer programming languages are better suited for the task than are others. The program will do a lot of file reading and even more pattern matching, so the best languages to use to produce the tool are those that are best at file handling and pattern matching.

Why use AWK?

AWK is a computer programming language designed to simplify file handling and pattern matching. In addition, the AWK language features automatic variable declarations, like BASIC, and dynamic named arrays unlike any other computer programming language.

One very powerful feature of AWK is that you can use a string for an array subscript. For example, if a file was to be searched and all occurrences of the words "President" and "fish" were to be counted, the AWK program illustrated in Fig. 13.1 could be used. The program tests each line read for one or more occurrences of each word. The program can find multiple occurrences of a single word in each line.

```
BEGIN {

WordCounter["President"] = 0
WordCounter["fish"] = 0
}

{
TestString = $0

while (match(TestString,"President")) {
      WordCounter["President"] += 1
      TestString = substr(TestString,RSTART+RLENGTH)
      }

TestString = $0;

while (match(TestString,"fish")) {
      WordCounter["fish"] += 1
      TestString = substr(TestString,RSTART+RLENGTH)
      }
}

END {

print "The word President was found ",
      WordCounter["President"],
      " times."
print "The word fish was found ",
      WordCounter["fish"],
      " times."
}
```

Figure 13.1   Example of "AWK" string array subscript use.

The program first reads a line from the file, represented by "$0". It then sets a variable "TestString" to equal the line from the file. The program searches the TestString for the pattern. If the pattern in found, the starting subscript in the line, (RSTART) and the length of the pattern (RLENGTH) are used to determine the starting subscript for the remainder of the string. The variable TestString is then reset to represent the remainder of the string. The loop continues searching TestString for the pattern until no match is found. The test string is then reset to the read line ("$0"), and a new loop entered checking for the second word. When the two-loop process is completed, the AWK program automatically reads the next line from the file and places it in "$0". The process repeats itself until the end of the file is found.

Coding style analysis

Each computer programming language has its own rules, regulations, and style. Depending upon the language in use, the variable declarations, naming conventions, and location in the source code will vary. The cross-reference generating program must be written to take such considerations into account.

In addition, many organizations have style requirements for program code modules. The requirements may be taken advantage of in a custom designed cross-reference generator to simplify information retrieval. For example, if a requirement is to list all modules referenced by a module in a comment block contained within the module, then the cross-reference generator can be made to seek out this comment block to obtain all necessary information.

To provide an example of coding style definitions, consider some coding style definitions for the C programming language. Refer to Fig. 13.2. The rules established are as follows:

1. All defined variable names are entirely upper case and are defined in an include file.

2. All defined data structures are mixed upper and lower case and are defined in an include file.

3. All external variables passed to or referenced in a function or procedure begin with an upper-case letter, all remaining characters are lower-case.

4. All local variables declared in a function or procedure are entirely lower-case.

While the above rules may or may not be appropriate for any given environment, they may be adapted and modified such that they are

```
#define MAX_CHARS 128
#define MAX_LINES 1024

typedef struct DATA {
        int             NumChars;
        char            HotChar;
        char            String[129];
        struct DATA     *NextDataStruct;
        } DataStruct;
```

Contents of "defines.c"

```
int defines(int Opcode)
{
int          index;
DataStruct   datablock;
```

. . . . .

Figure 13.2   Contents of "defines.h".

logical and easy to implement in the environment in which they are used. Using rules similar to the above rules provides an easy way to identify classes of variables and to process them accordingly when constructing a cross-reference. For example, when constructing a data impact statement, there is no need to cross-reference the local variables. However, data structures do need to be cross-referenced and can be readily identified by the leading upper-case character.

Designing the cross-reference database

There are many ways to create and use database files. It is beyond the scope of this book to describe how such mechanisms came into being and list their benefits and drawbacks. The actual design of the database, in terms of content and storage, is left to the reader. The issues herein discussed concern design methodology.

Producing a cross-reference is a two-step process. First, all modules must be searched for appropriate data, either function reference or data use, and a record produced for each module. The next step is to take the generated data and compile it into a single reference file, the cross-reference database.

A simple database can be constructed and all such entries put into the database by the developer. However, the accuracy of such a database depends upon the developer updating the database for any change. Secondly, the process of adding such information to a database is an additional duty that many programmers will shirk. It could be very difficult to get such a database into operation, much less maintain it. A better solution is to employ an automated cross-reference generator.

One common method used for cross-reference generation is to create a cross-reference generator that produces a single flat file record for each module during the first pass. Then, periodically, all of these single-record files are read by a program that collects and collates the data. Because there may be hundreds of modules, there may be hundreds of single-record files and the periodic compilation of the accumulated data may take considerable time. Perhaps a more efficient method might be to create a multiple-record file for each source directory. The compiling program would then read the directory file rather than multiple module files, thus enhancing the performance of the compiling program.

Constructing the database generator

Whatever language or database system is in use, the program should be able to produce variable-length records. For example, if the cross-reference generator is used to produce a data impact statement, then each data type will have a number of modules listed that make use of the data type. The number of modules will vary from one data type to another.

Another issue is that the generation of a cross-reference is a two-step process. This two-step requirement is not a problem if a computer programming language is used to produce the cross-reference generator, it may be an issue if a standard database system is used.

Finally, to accomplish such a task, the language or system used may or may not be difficult to program. If no language or system has been specified for use, then selection should be based upon portability, ease of use, and required effort. If the organization has not considered using AWK, it may well be a good solution. AWK is portable and runs on DOS, OS/2, and many UNIX systems. AWK is easy to learn and use. Finally, AWK was designed with pattern-matching and file-handling as the primary programming requirements, thus the effort to produce a cross-reference in AWK may take far less time than using some other computer programming language with which the developer might be familiar.

Automating the database construction

There are several ways to automate the construction of the cross-reference database. The common bond between all of the methods is that they are all invoked, either by hand or from some other process, such as a running build script. A build script whose sole purpose is to construct the cross-reference listing can be constructed. With such a build script, the cross-reference generation is automated. When the cross-reference is constructed by hand, it is not.

It may be that reconstruction of the database is desired every time a new revision is checked in. This may be a little extreme. However, to do so, a special build script can be produced that checks in a new revision and invokes the cross-reference generator programs. A better build script would generate the first-pass information for the newly checked-in module and compare the new information to that previously produced. Only if a difference is detected in the module information would the second-pass cross-reference generation program be invoked.

Generating the Where Used Document

Recall that a where used document is a listing of all modules that call a given module. Therefore, the production of the cross-reference database is at least a two-step process. If the cross-reference is to contain only defined function and procedure names and not standard library calls, the first thing to produce is a list of all the function and procedure names. The list is produced by examining each module and extracting the names of any declared functions or procedures. Once the list has been generated, it must be incorporated into the program that will do the module search and construct the cross-reference database. During the search, each module is examined to determine the names of the functions and procedures that the module calls. After each module is examined, the module name is written to the database. Immediately following the module name, the names of all the functions and procedures it calls or references are listed. Refer to Fig. 13.3. The module names are even with the left margin, the referenced functions and procedures are indented with a tab. When using a programming

```
ModuleA
        Function_1
        Function_2
        Function_3

ModuleB
        Function_2
        Function_4
        Procedure_1

ModuleC
        Function_1
        Function_3
        Procedure_2
        Procedure_3
```

Figure 13.3   Example "where used" database file contents.

language such as AWK, it is easy to separate the module names from the references because of the leading tab character in the lines that name the referenced function or procedure.

Searching the database

Once the single-file database has been constructed, it can be searched for module names. The search will be invoked with the name of the function or procedure of interest. The objective is to find all modules that reference the named function or procedure. As the database file is processed, each time a new module name is encountered the name of the module is stored in a temporary variable. The functions and procedures referenced by the module are then examined. If a match between the named function or procedure and one of the referenced functions or procedures is found, then the module name is added to a list of modules that reference the named function or procedure.

Constructing the document builder

The output format of the document builder is completely arbitrary and up to the designer and his or her peers and managers. Because the report is largely utilitarian in purpose, it may not be worth a lot of trouble to add fancy fonts and formatting to the report. The document builder can be integrated into the database search engine and a simple report produced that lists the named function or procedure followed by the names of all the modules that reference it.

Generating the Data Impact Statement

Generating the data impact statement is similar in nature to generating the where used document in that all the source code must be searched. The difference is that instead of looking for function and procedure calls, the database generator is looking for data structures.

Most computer languages have a specific location in the code body for data-type declarations. In some languages, data types are declared in include files. For functions and procedures, the data types used by the function are declared when the function is declared. In some languages, such as "C++", data declarations can be anywhere in the code body. Whatever the case may be, a given set of keywords that identify data types can be constructed by combining the data types native to the language with the data types declared in the include files.

The object here is to find the names of the modules that make use of a specified data type. Normally, it is only user-defined data types that are of concern as they can be redefined, native data types cannot.

When debugging, it is reasonable to include native data types in your reports as it may well be that an alteration of a return value is the cause for all of the dismay.

Constructing the database

Constructing the database for the data impact statement is accomplished in much the same manner as for the where used document. The first thing that needs to be done is to determine the names of the data types. For the purposes of this discussion, assume that only user-defined data types are to be referenced. The source code and the include files must be searched for data-type declarations. These are usually identified by keywords such as *"record", "typedef", "struct"*, or *"class"*. As the search progresses, each new data type is added to an array of data types. When the search is complete, a file is written that contains the list of data types.

The next step is to produce a list of the module names that reference each data type. As each source code module is processed, the name of the module is added to a data-type array when the module uses that data type. When the search is complete, a file is written with a listing of modules by data type. In AWK, C, or whatever other computer language you are using, an array of character strings is created for each data type. This is simplest in AWK because in AWK a dynamic character array may have a "name" and the AWK code is easy and simple to write. In C or most any other computer language, an object or structure containing a string array for the data name and a pointer to an object that identifies a module can be produced. The second object contains a module name and a pointer to another module-naming object, (see Fig. 13.4). The effort involved in producing such a report generator is far greater. The program must be able to read the first list, the data type names, and create a linked list of objects for each data type on the fly. The task in producing code to do this is not difficult,

```
typedef struct MODULENAME {
        char                    ModuleName[13];
        struct MODULENAME       *NextModuleName;

        } ModuleName;

typedef struct DATATYPELIST {
        char                    DataObjectName[32];
        ModuleName              *ModuleNames;
        } DataTypeList;
```

Figure 13.4 "C" code data structures for producing "data impact document."

just very time consuming. Why reinvent the wheel? If you are not an AWK fanatic it is probably due to under-exposure. Those who know the language, love the language.

One way to organize the database file is to place the data type names flush with no margin and to indent the module names list by a space or tab character, as shown in Fig. 13.5. The starting character is then used to identify the lines that contain module names. All data type names are identified because they start flush with the margin and have no identifying character.

Searching the database

Searching the database is a simple task. A program can be written that allows the user to specify the name of the data type to search for. The program then searches the file, wherein modules are listed under data type, for the correct data type and then prints the associated module list. For example, a program can be written, call it *DataUsed*, that is invoked with a list of data type names as parameters. An invocation from the command line might look like:

    DataUsed ModuleName DataTypeList.

The program then reads the database file, searching for either specified data type, in this case, "ModuleName" or a data type specified in "DataTypeList".

Retrieving the desired information

When one of the data type names specified by the user is found, the name of the data type and the names of all the modules that reference that data type are printed. They continue to print until the program

"0" column

```
ModuleName
    BldDBase
    WriteList
    ReadModule
DataTypeList
    BldDBase
    WriteList
    ReadModule
    GenDataUseReport
```

Figure 13.5 Module listing by data type.

reads a new line that begins with something other than the character that identifies the line as containing a module name.

Formatting the output

As in the where used document, the content of the data impact statement is far more important than the format of the content. The document is utilitarian in nature. However, it may well be that for some reason or another, a pretty format for the report is required. If the report generator was written in AWK, then formatting the output into a desired look is very easy. AWK provides several mechanisms by which the output of the program can be formatted into exactly the look that is desired.

Summary

The impact analysis process can be used to generate two types of reports, the where used document and the data impact statement. The *where used document* specifies the names of modules that invoke a specified module. The *data impact statement* specifies the names of modules that use a specified data type. Both of these reports are especially useful in the software engineering environment.

Questions

1. How would you write a where used document generator in your favorite language?

2. Write a function to count the number of times the words "President" and "fish" appear in an ASCII file. Use your favorite language. Compare your program with the AWK example in Fig. 13.1. How does it compare? Which would be easier to use to if you had to generate a data impact statement?

14

Mainframe Versus Network Development

While a mainframe and a distributed computer network have many things in common, there are vast differences between the two environments when software development is considered. Often, a person from the mainframe environment will think that because both systems serve multiple users and they both store data, they are similar enough for mainframe techniques to work on networks of personal computers. However, this is not true. Not only are there differences in the mechanical natures of the two environments, but the software that runs on the two different machine types is completely different. Solutions that work on a mainframe may not work in a network environment.

Similarities

Both the mainframe and the LAN file server have many similarities. Both service multiple users. Both provide file storage and retrieval services. Both require configuration management for development. Both the mainframe and the network file server have one or more central processing units dedicated to serving the users. However, the list of similarities is much smaller than the list of differences.

Differences

The mainframe computer has a single set of one or more central processing units whose resources are shared among all the users. When a user invokes a word-processing package, the mainframe's central processing unit runs the word-processing program on a time-shared basis. The program takes up some of the mainframe's system memory. In fact, a vast research program came up with the idea of the "sticky bit," where a program is loaded into main memory and is then shared by all users that invoke it, just to save on system memory consumption. Because the use of the central processing unit is time-shared, each user receives a slice of the central processing unit's overall cycles. If the user is considering what to write next, the mainframes central processing unit still checks to see if there is any character input each time it is that user's time slice. The central processing unit must save its current context, load the user's context, check for input, save the user's context, and move on to the next user's context. Many expensive central processing unit cycles are wasted during each context switch.

A network of personal computers has many sets of central processing units. The file server has a set of one or more central processing units. Each personal computer or workstation has its own central processing unit. The file server's central processing unit is dedicated to maintaining network communications and transmitting and receiving data from the individual workstations. When a user invokes a word-processing program on a network, the file server downloads the program to the local workstation. Once the program is downloaded, the file server is done. The actual program runs on the workstation. The advantage here is that a very inexpensive processor is dedicated to the needs of just one person. Now, if the user is contemplating a new report, the only central processing unit that is wasting cycles is the inexpensive central processing unit in the workstation. The file server does not spend any cycles at all during this pause.

When a mainframe computer serves many users, the performance realized by each individual is sometimes hard to call *performance*. This is because the resources of the one central processing unit are being shared by many people. Each user's time slice becomes further and further apart as more users log on to the system.

Because the central processing unit of the workstation is dedicated to the user, the user will never see a degradation in performance as more and more people log into the network. True, the network itself may slow down due to traffic, but that will have no impact upon the user using his or her word processor. The networked workstation will never be as slow as the mainframe when many users are on the system. The mainframe must communicate with each terminal to check for input. The network must communicate with workstations, but only upon request.

Performance aside, perhaps the biggest difference between the mainframe environment and the network environment is cost. A typical mainframe computer environment may cost upwards from $6,000,000, for the mainframe, require well over $10,000 a month in maintenance and environmental controls, and approximately $5000 for each terminal and its communications links. A recent study performed at a major banking institution found that the CPU charges alone for each developer were approximately $90,000 per year. Including depreciation and other related costs, over $125,000 a year is spent providing the developer with the hardware required to perform his or her assigned duties. This does not include the cost of software, which is very expensive for mainframe computers.

This same institution found that by moving to networked personal computers, the reduction in cost was staggering. The network server, including all the software applications that they needed, cost approximately $45,000. Each workstation cost approximately $7000 and included tape backup, disk drives, and graphical output that they could not possibly get with their mainframe terminals. The cost per developer was less than $3000 per year computed on a three year investment cycle, including software.

Anyone who tells you that three equals one hundred twenty-five is someone who cannot count. By moving to a personal computer network development system, not only did the organization save approximately $122,000 per year, per programmer, but their productivity nearly doubled. Because the developers were no longer waiting on the mainframe for responses, they were saving time and money!

In the land of dollars and cents, it is easy to see the vast difference between the two environments. A ten-person team working for a year on the mainframe computer to develop a system would cost over $1,250,000 in hardware charges. The same ten-person team working in a personal computer network environment would finish the same project in six months at a cost of just over $15,000 in hardware and software charges.

Nearly every mainframe-based application is character-based. The user can run one program on his or her terminal and it occupies the entire screen. Even though the mainframe is a multitasking, multiuser machine, the individual user sees a single task on his or her terminal. Graphical user interfaces, graphical representations, flow charts, data flow diagrams, and a host of other useful user tools are just not widely available to the mainframe computer user. Most terminals will not support graphical output of any kind, much less multiple text-editing windows. On the other hand, almost every personal computer workstation is equipped with an inexpensive graphical display device. It is very hard to purchase a workstation that does not have a graphical display device. Personal computer and workstation programs take advantage of this ability to provide the graphical user interface, graphical representations, multicolored graphical output, and of course, multiple text editing windows.

The mainframe user who wishes to copy a segment of code from one module to another must merge the two modules and then delete the extra material. The workstation user merely copies the text from one text-editing window and pastes it into another text-editing window. The mainframe user who wishes to compare two sections of code must obtain hard copy, even if the two sections are in the same module. The workstation user can open two windows on the same document and position the desired sections in each window so that the comparison can occur on-screen. The workstation user can open two windows and compare line-by-line two different modules, on-screen.

Yet another difference between the two system types is that on the mainframe all files are located in one place. On most networks, the files can be located in one of many places. Networks often have more than one file server. In fact, some networks allow each workstation to act as a file server to the extent that any one workstation on the network can access files located on any other workstation. The mainframe has a single data set, the network can have multiple data sets.

Finally, one last difference between the mainframe computer and the network of personal computer workstations. The operating system running on the mainframe was designed with multiuser capabilities and safeguards built in. The operating system running on most personal computer workstations was designed for a single user and has no multiuser safeguards built in. True, the network file server has multiuser safeguards, but they are of a different nature than those on the mainframe. They are different because the power of the central processing unit is different and because the tasks run by the operating systems on each type machine are different. The mainframe must be able to run word processors along with transaction-analysis software along with database software, and so on. The network file server has one task and one task only to perform, manage the network communications, including data transfers.

How the Differences Affect the CM Paradigm

Mainframe developers work in an environment designed specifically for developers. From the first time they join a development team and write their first lines of code, they are locked into the current system. They must comply with the configuration management tools and rules as implemented on the machine if they wish to do any work at all. In essence, mainframe developers are forced to use the tools.

The personal computer, on the other hand, has no such environment provided. Personal computer developers may successfully develop applications without ever using any configuration management tools at all. This is even true in a network of personal computer workstations. Developers in the network environment, must learn to use the tools, learn why they should use the tools, and be guided by the tools into their proper use. This basic difference in the two environments has only been addressed in recent years with such products as the PVCS Version Manager.

One of the differences between the environments addressed above is the manner in which data is stored. The mainframe has centralized data storage, all files are stored on the mainframe. The network allows users to store files both on the server and on the workstation. While this difference may not seem major in nature, it causes profound differences in the way that files are maintained by the configuration management software.

Because of the way in which mainframe configuration management systems work, often, managers from the mainframe environment feel that it is necessary to maintain two sets of archive files on the network. The first is the development set, the second is the set of all releases. This is the so-called *physical promotion model*. This is not necessary. The proper use of version labels overcomes the difficulties as perceived by those managers in maintaining release control. Perhaps a better method would be to maintain the network archive files as suggested in this book and by the developers of the PVCS product series and to maintain the mainframe version control strictly for releases. The network version of the archive files stores all information, including releases (via a version label) and new production releases are uploaded to the mainframe to be stored in whatever version control software system is in use on the mainframe. This is the *logical promotion model*.

Summary

All in all, the differences between configuration management on the mainframe and on a network of personal computer workstations are not vast and do not cause incompatibilities. The real difference lies in how the tools are designed and used and, as a result, how the overall configuration management system is implemented. While some mainframe techniques may work on personal computer networks, they may not be the best techniques to use. If you are a mainframe developer or manager, talk to someone with some good experience in the network environment before you implement the mainframe policy on the network. You may save yourself a lot of grief and you may even learn something new and completely out of the range of your experiences on the mainframe.

Questions

1. What other differences can you name between the mainframe and networked personal computer environments?

2. The mainframe paradigm has always been to get as much use out of the CPU cycles as is possible. That is the reason batch processing was invented. The workstation grew from a processing unit that had very limited capabilities. Limited instructions and very small memory space were major concerns when dealing with microprocessors. The paradigm was to get as much as possible out of the minimal resources and to use those resources in a creative fashion. How does the difference in paradigm affect the way in which programs are designed for each of the two environments?

15

Network Development of Mainframe Applications

Because of the vast cost differential in developing applications on the mainframe versus the local area network, much of the development effort is moving into the network environment. Not only is development moving toward the network, some applications as well are migrating into the multiprocessor environment provided by networks.

Downsizing

The latest trend in the mainframe development is downsizing (or right-sizing). This trend began just several years ago with the advent of large scale local area networks and powerful personal computers. Downsizing makes sense in a lot of ways, it provides a less expensive development environment and removes the burden of development from the mainframe, thus freeing the mainframe to do the work it was designed and programmed to do.

In some instances, downsizing means removing the mainframe completely from the application environment. A network server coupled with multiple data-entry personal computer workstations can often replace the mainframe completely in some applications where the computational and transactional power of the mainframe is not required.

There are several driving factors that are pushing the acceptance of downsizing. The primary reason that downsizing will become more acceptable and found in more organizations is financial in nature. Another reason is the richness of the personal computer tool sets.

Financial factors

There are several financial factors that are of great importance to any development organization. The cost of the equipment that is used to develop the application, the cost of the equipment used to run the application, and the nonrecurring engineering costs associated with developing the application.

Regardless of the equipment used when developing an application, the actual work involved is quite similar. Files are edited, compilations occur, tests are made, and so on. The cost of a single mainframe computer is far greater than that of a local area network, yet the development tasks for each environment are essentially identical. If a development effort uses 30 percent of a mainframe's resources, then the mainframe's ability to perform application tasks is reduced by that thirty percent. If the mainframe computer's yearly amortization and maintenance costs are $1,000,000 per year, then approximately $300,000 a year would be spent on nonrevenue-generating development activities. This drives up the cost of the service provided by the mainframe computer, which in turn is passed on to the customer. The additional costs make competitiveness a difficult goal. In the future, development on the mainframe may prove to be prohibitively expensive.

If a company spends upwards of $10,000,000 on a computer, then each and every cycle of the machine's central processing unit is truly expensive. If a machine is purchased to run a given application set, then it seems silly to waste a large percentage of those expensive machine cycles just waiting for character input from each user. When developers are creating an application on a mainframe computer, an extremely large percentage of the computer's machine cycles are dedicated to text editing. Most of those machine cycles are wasted waiting for character input and performing context switching between users.

As the power of the file server increases over time, more an more applications that required a mainframe to run will be able to migrate to the lower-cost network environment. In some cases, only the development effort will move to the network. In others, the entire system will migrate to the network.

When the entire application migrates downward, some changes in characteristics are to be expected. There may or may not be a performance hit to a mainframe application when it is run on a client-server local area network. Not all applications will take a performance hit, some may actually experience a performance gain. Whether or not there is a performance loss or gain depends upon the structure of the application. Applications that are user-interaction-driven will experience a performance gain when moved to the local area network.

Applications that are transaction-driven or database intensive may experience a performance loss. However, even if a loss of performance is experienced, when the performance degradation percentage is compared to the cost differential, it becomes quite easy to adjust to the performance hit.

If you reduce the cost of the development environment, you automatically reduce the cost of developing an application. By moving application development to a local area network, the mainframe computer is relieved of the development task. If the mainframe computer was near the limits of its performance when handling both the development effort and the running of applications, then offloading the development effort will free up enough of the CPU cycle workload so that the mainframe will no longer be stretched to its limits. In cases where the purchase of a second or third mainframe computer just to handle the work load seems imminent, downsizing the development effort may alleviate the need for additional processing power and save the expense of purchasing another mainframe computer. By spending a few thousand dollars on a local area network and workstations, the company may save more than a few million dollars.

Productivity aspects

Another aspect of downsizing the development organization is that productivity will increase. Because each user has a dedicated central processing unit waiting for every character that they enter, the user loses no time waiting for character-read and character-screen update from the mainframe. With downsizing, the mainframe computer no longer is spending a significant amount of time swapping context between users just to determine whether or not a user has pressed a key. Workstation users see immediate feedback. Mainframe users must sometimes wait for several seconds to see that same feedback.

While several seconds of waiting does not appear to be a long time in itself, recall that those seconds are wasted for each character typed in a day, week, year, and so on. If a person types ten thousand characters a day, and each character requires a half second wait, then the person is losing five thousand seconds a day waiting on the character-input, character-output loop. Five thousand seconds a day is equal to 1.39 hours a day, 6.95 hours a week, and 361.4 hours a year. At a burdened cost of $150.00 per hour, the company is loosing $54,210.00 per year, per person.

In the development arena, typing is important, but the real time-consuming tasks are compilation and linkage. A 40-min compile on a workstation has no impact whatsoever on the file server. A 40-min compile on a mainframe may impact every other user adversely, with an equal, if not greater, impact on any applications running on the mainframe. Every mainframe developer has watched their terminal appear to go to sleep for prolonged periods of time, time that could have been put to use if the user was working on a personal computer or workstation.

Every minute wasted on waiting for computer response drives up the cost of the development effort. Because of the relative low cost of local area networks, in a few more years very little development will be conducted on the mainframe computer. Development will migrate to the local area network.

Control aspects

The perception that a lot of tiny computers tied to a small computer presents an uncontrollable environment is one factor that will slow the migration from the mainframe to the local area network. This perception is in error. The methods differ, but the controls are present. A lot of time and money was spent in producing the controls and tools that exist on the mainframe today. These same controls and tools are migrating to the local area network. The PVCS tool set is an example of this migration. In fact, PVCS was conceived and developed for LAN-based development. With a little effort and thought, the same safe environment that exists on the mainframe can be implemented on the local area network.

Platform considerations

One large consideration in downsizing is maintaining the ability to port an application to various platforms. Very few mainframe computers are identical to one another. Even mainframe computers from the same manufacturer may differ considerably. Any given mainframe application may need to run on 10 or more different mainframe platforms.

The ability of the PVCS Version Manager to provide archive file branches, coupled with the branch development environment provided by the PVCS Version Manager, greatly simplifies the migration of multiple-platform application development to the local area network. Figure 15.1 illustrates an archive file of one module of just such an application. The application is developed for one platform. When it is stabilized on that platform, the stable revision of the module is branched with one branch for each additional desired supported platform. All modules are branched in such a fashion. The result is that the tip revision of each branch represents the application port to the respec-

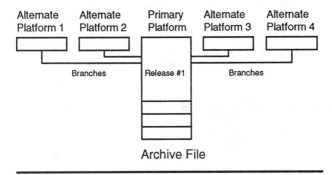

Figure 15.1   Multiple-platform release.

tive platform represented by the branch. The DefaultVersion, BaseVersion, and BranchVersion directives simplify managing the development environment. While many programmers may use the same BaseVersion revisions, they may each use completely different DefaultVersion and BranchVersion directives. Thus, while the root of all the branches is the same, the actual branch that each programmer works on by default, without any difference in commands issued by the programmers, will be a different branch of the same archive file.

When the application development enters another iteration, development for the primary platform can commence as if no branches were present. The developers of the new release need not be aware of the branches or of the alternate platforms to be supported. When the next release of the application is ready, the newly-released revisions can be automatically merged with the branch revisions of the previous release. The merge program "VMERGE" will flag all differences between two revisions of the same module so that the programmer does not have to search for the differences, just resolve them. Once the differences have been resolved, a new branch can be started from the new release revision. Figure 15.2 illustrates an archive file that has undergone two releases for five different platforms.

The merge program compares two revisions against a revision common to both revisions and produces a combined working copy with both sets of changes. The relationships between the revisions are illustrated in Fig. 15.3. The core of the common revision is kept in the new working copy of the module. Any section in the two merged revisions that differs from the common source is included in the new working copy. Any place where both revisions differ from the source, and the changes are not identical between the revisions, both sets of changes are included in the working copy. In this case the differences are flagged by the merge program. The merge program does not resolve the differences as it knows nothing about computer languages, much

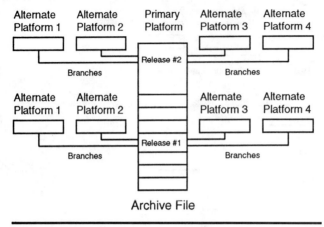

Figure 15.2 Multiple-platform multiple release.

less what the module is trying to accomplish. The resolution of the differences is left to the developer who does know such things.

The Network-Mainframe Interface

Other than a communications interface by which code can be up- and downloaded, there must, at a minimum, be a release-level interface between the local area network and the mainframe computer if the application developed on the local area network is to run on the mainframe. Some division of labor in an organized, planned, and logical manner must be achieved. The mainframe application must be kept in synchronization with the releases of the application made on the local area network.

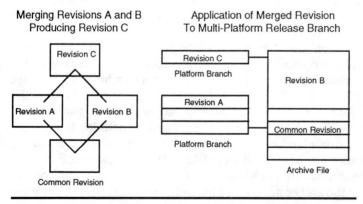

Figure 15.3 Using merge to update multiplatform releases.

Downsizing does not imply that the tools and methods used on the mainframe are discarded and never used again. In reality, both sets of tools, those on the mainframe and those on the local area network, should work in concert. One does not replace the other. True, the mainframe tools can be used to control the network development effort, but at a cost of considerable up- and downloading and the potential for grave errors on the network side. The danger lies in the fact that the network environment would then be subject to human error, so mistakes might happen that could jeopardize the development effort. It would be far better to use configuration management techniques in both environments.

Reduction of mainframe CM responsibilities

When a local area network is used to develop mainframe applications, the day-by-day maintenance of revisions is controlled by the configuration management software running on the network file server, for example, PVCS. The mainframe no longer has to maintain these minor changes. In addition, the mainframe is no longer required to track the progression of the modules through the various promotion groups.

What is done on the network?

The local area network tracks the day-by-day module changes as well as the promotion of the revisions from development all the way through final test and release. Testing and verification are first conducted on the network version of the application. All test suites, test programs, documentation, and any other related file types are stored on the network file server and under the file server's configuration management software. Virtually all development tracking that was performed on the mainframe computer can be used on the local area network.

What is maintained on the mainframe?

Once a release is made from the local area network development environment, the new release is uploaded to the mainframe computer and recompiled. The new revisions of the source modules associated with the new release should be stored in the mainframe's configuration management software as they were before the downsizing took place. Using this policy, it is very easy to back out a new release if it proves to be flawed. The old code does not need to be uploaded as it is already stored on the mainframe. Recovery time is minimized.

Storing released revisions on the mainframe also has an additional benefit. Many old-time mainframe developers and managers feel a lot more secure knowing that the mainframe has the ability to revert to prior releases without the need to obtain older code from another environment. Knowing that the application works on the mainframe, and assurance that the exact copy of the code used to make the working program is readily available reduces stress. The mainframe manager does not need to be concerned with the ability of the local area network to provide his or her mainframe with the correct code.

Tests, test data, and test suites that can only be run on the mainframe are also stored under the mainframe's configuration management environment. Although, just like development, perhaps only the current release and a prior release of the tests, test data, and test suites are stored on the mainframe.

Mapping Mainframe Strategies and Tools to the LAN

There are some strategies, tools, and methods that have been in use on mainframe computers for many years. Some of these will map readily to the network environment. Others will not. Those that do not map on a one-to-one basis may be implemented on the network with a little consideration and thought.

The copy book

A *copy book* is a collection of information, or data set, that is referenced by one or more applications. The copy book is subject to change as is any data set. It may prove important to match the version of a copy book with a version of an application. Usually, the records contained within a copy book do not change scope. That is, the record structure and the quality and type of data stored in a record are usually fixed for some duration of time. Most frequently, it is the quantity of records that changes. If the scope of the copy book changes, then an older application may not run with the new version of the copy book.

When a new version of a copy book is created, it is really a new revision of the same file. The new version can be checked in with an appropriate identifying version label. If an application requires a specific version of a copy book, then the application can be made to obtain the correct version. Refer to Fig. 15.4. The application can make system calls to the operating system to check out the correct version of the copy book and then open and access the newly created copy of the copy book.

Psuedo Language Example

```
System("get -w -vVERSION_10 CopyBook.Dat");

Open ("CopyBook.Dat","READ_ONLY");

Process ("CopyBook.Dat");

Close ("CopyBook.Dat");

System("del CopyBook.Dat");

End (Application)
```

Figure 15.4   Obtaining the correct version of a copy book.

The librarian

The *librarian* is a system by which tested and completed modules can be accessed by a linkage editor when constructing an application. In the mainframe world, the librarian provides much more functionality than this. In fact, the librarian and the repository, discussed in the next section, are very similar in function. Because the distinction is somewhat vague depending upon whom it is defined by, we will define the librarian as above. This definition of a librarian can be mapped to the object-file librarian in the personal computer development arena. In practice, the personal computer object-file librarian is used to construct libraries of object files associated with a specific function or application. For example, a collection of modules that are used to create a graphical user interface can be compiled and the resultant object files can be combined into a single library file called "gui.lib". Once a library has been created, any application can link in object-file members from the library.

The repository

For our purpose in drawing a distinction between a librarian and a repository, a repository is defined as follows. A *repository* is a collection of one or more files whose contents track the revisions of source code and other file types. In some cases, a single file is used for the repository. However, in the network development arena, it is better to use the distributed database structure such as is implemented in the PVCS tool set's archive file database. The mainframe repository maps to the network-based archive file data set.

One reason the distributed database paradigm is preferred in the network development environment is that the searches made thereof can be controlled and thus faster. By setting the VCSDir configuration parameter, the regions of the database that are to be searched can be limited. Thus, the search mechanism can complete its search after examining a limited set of module declarations rather than the complete list of all existing modules.

Summary

The primary driving force in the downsizing trend is expense. A network file server with multiple networked workstations is far less expensive than a mainframe computer. Additional benefits are the productivity gain realized by users having their own dedicated central processing unit and access to a far richer tool set.

Questions

1. Developing an application that is meant to run on a mainframe computer in the network environment has some risks. What potential pitfalls are there and how could they be avoided? Is there a situation in which downsizing is not practical? Why or why not?

2. If access to a mainframe computer site can be gained, determine the yearly maintenance charges. How much does maintaining the environment cost? How much does down time cost?

3. If access to a network site is possible, determine the yearly maintenance cost. Is a controlled environment necessary as with the mainframe? What impact does server down time have? How does it affect the workstations? Can the workstation user continue to work if the network is down? Can a mainframe user continue to work if the mainframe goes down?

16

Developing a
Project Hierarchy

Every application program has a design. Data must flow properly and be processed in a controlled and correct manner. Each application has subsystems. As illustrated in Fig. 16.1, an example of a three-section application, one section of an application may be dedicated to user interaction, another to processing data, and another to communications. The natural division of an application in terms of a project hierarchy is along the sectional borders.

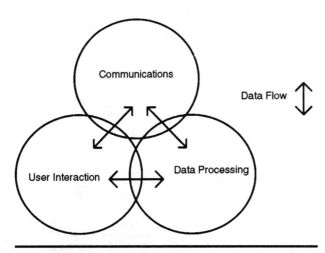

Figure 16.1   A three-section application.

A Functional Perspective

Each section of an application has a specific purpose or function. Each of the application subsystems may in turn have subsystems of their own. Using the example of a three-section application shown in Fig. 16.1, assume that the user-interaction section consists of an additional three subsystems, keyboard input, mouse input, and screen drawing. Further, assume that the data-processing section consists of two subsystems, adding records and sorting records, and that the communications subsystems consists of three subsystems, writing files, reading files, and external communications. In this case, a project hierarchy may appear as illustrated in Fig. 16.2. The hierarchy of the project is reflected in the directories wherein the related files are stored.

A Type-Based Perspective

Once the lowest level of section has been identified, then that section may be further divided into a type-based directory structure. While further division may not be practical in the working environment, it may be very useful to further divide the configuration management files. Each section that has one or more include files may have an include directory in addition to directories for each source code type,

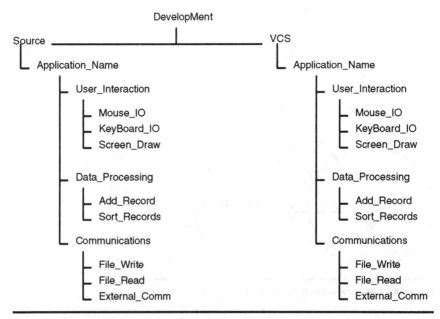

Figure 16.2   Project hierarchy implemented as directories.

(for example C-code and Assembly-code). In Fig. 16.3, the project-wide include files are stored in a subdirectory directly under the project's main (application) directory. The include files are stored in a subdirectory of the highest level directory under which all other subdirectories contain one or more modules that reference the stored include file.

Configuration files for lower-level subsystems under which no further subsystems are defined may be appropriate for use of the FirstMatch directive. The FirstMatch directive causes PVCS to stop a search for a file type once a directory that contains files of the same type has been encountered. For example, assume the VCSDir configuration file directive specified in a local configuration file is: "VCSDir=C:\vcs\project\include;C:\vcs\project\cobol". Assume that the first directory, "C:\vcs\project\include" contains archive files with the file suffix ".INV". Further assume that an include file "FINDME.INC" has an archive file "FINDME.INV" that resides in the directory "C:\vcs\project\cobol". If a user specifies FirstMatch in their local configuration file and then attempts to perform an operation on the archive file "FINDME.INV", the operation will fail. PVCS will find ".INV" files in the directory "C:\vcs\project\include" and will stop the search after examining that directory.

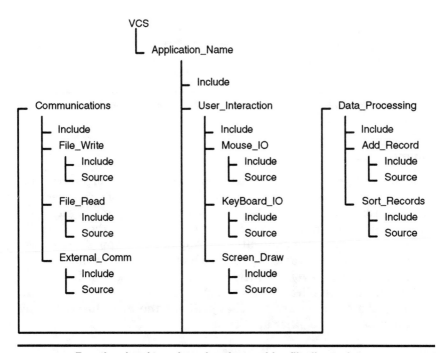

Figure 16.3 Functional and type-based project archive file directories.

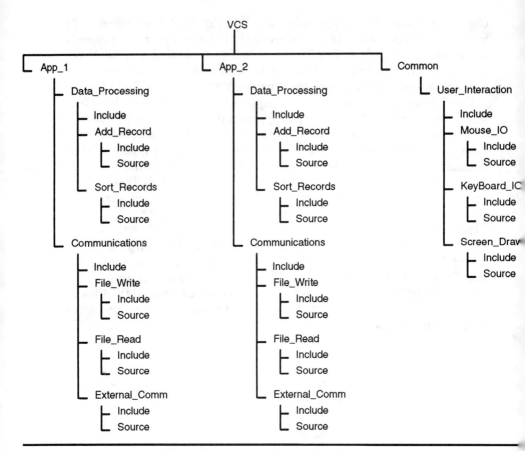

Figure 16.4   Application specific and common function archive file directories.

Commonalties

Some subsystems of an application may apply to one or more other applications. If more than one application makes use of a code section, then the archive files for that section should be stored at a higher level in the archive file directory tree. Figure 16.4 illustrates the archive file directory tree when two applications, "App_1" and "App_2" make use of the same user interface subsystems which are stored in the common directory at a peer-level with the application directories. Using this method reduces duplication and complexity. Each application can reference the common archive files without the need to access the directory space of the other application.

Summary

The project hierarchy is a variable concept whose implementation is dependent upon the nature of the environment and the function classes of the code subsystems. The overall hierarchy is dependent upon the number of projects and the nature and function of common elements.

Questions

1. Assume that a project hierarchy has been defined. If examination of the hierarchy proves that the development effort could be better served by alteration of the hierarchy, how difficult would it be to alter the hierarchy? What steps would be taken? How could you ensure the success of the effort?

2. Describe an environment in which use of the "FirstMatch" directive would not be beneficial. Is such an environment common? Why?

17

Managing Reusable Code

One benefit obtained from practicing configuration management techniques is a truly maintainable and reusable program component or object. Instead of writing a commonly-used function over and over again, perhaps once for each application, the function is written once and reused. Once a reusable program object has been created and stored, it can be used by any application that requires the functionality of that object.

Many existing program modules are probably candidates for becoming reusable objects. Any piece of code that conforms to a specification that defines a single basic procedure or function can be established as a reusable program object. For example, a function to set the date or time or a procedure that provides basic file input/output operations would be a good candidate. A procedure that performs specific application tasks, such as a parser, is not a good candidate for reuse.

To illustrate the creation and maintenance of a reusable program object, we will define, create and store a reusable object. The object of our creation will be a program module whose function is to return the average value of a variable number of integers. As we do so, we will create specifications and code. The specifications will illustrate a minimalist approach to forms and information content. We will provide only the bare essentials. There are many more fields that could be created and, not only may they be necessary in a given situation, many of them should be used. For example, here are a few that should be used in any specification, project name, project leader, engineer, designer, programmer, author, manager, and project manager.

Creating the Reusable Object

The first task in the reusable object creation process is producing the requirements specification. The requirements specification defines the purpose for the module. Thus the requirements specification is the module's basic definition. Figure 17.1 illustrates the requirements specification for the averaging function we wish to construct. Additional information that could be contained on the form would be the name of the initiating project and the library in which the module will be stored. The fundamental reason for the existence of the document is that a requirements specification spells out exactly what the function is to do.

The next step is to create the functional specification. Contained in the functional specification are all the properties or attributes of the module. These attributes are its return value, all parameters that are passed to the module, the return value of the module and its internal variables. Figure 17.2 illustrates a minimal functional specification.

Once the functional specification is accomplished, a pseudo-code module, similar to Fig. 17.3, might be produced. Depending upon the environment and the nature of the module, a pseudocode module may or may not be useful. If a pseudocode module is used, then in some cases, the pseudocode version of the module is considered revision 0.0. However, if pseudocode modules are used, then consider also that they are subject to change just as often as the specification is altered. A good specification should remain fairly static, but that is no guarantee that it will not change. If feasible, pseudocode modules should be maintained in their own archive files.

Figure 17.4 shows the averaging module implemented in the C programming language. Note that the illustration contains no comment lines. In a real life situation, this would be unacceptable. No matter how simple the module, some form of documentation must accompany the source code. A reader must be able to determine what is going on in the code. Variable names should specify exactly what they represent. A nested loop should have counters named something like "outer_loop_counter" and "inner_loop_counter" or almost any other identifier rather than "i" and "j."

Tasks:

1.   Determine the number of integers to average.

2.   Sum the integers, storing the running sum internally.

3.   Divide the sum by the number of integers.

4.   Return the result.

Figure 17.1   Requirements specification.

Name:
>   Var_Int_Average().

Definition:
>   A function to average a variable number of integer values.

Passed Parameters:
>   An integer representing the number of integer values.
>   A pointer to an array of integers.

Return Value:
>   An integer representing the average.

Internal Variables:
>   An integer to represent the running sum.
>   An internal counter.

Figure 17.2   Functional specification.

Storing the Reusable Object

Once a fully coded module's correctness has been proven, the module's authors have the right to declare the object reusable. This does not say that the module is perfect in every way. Perhaps some oddity in the compiler converts a long integer into a short integer before converting it back into a long integer for some obscure reason. It has been known to happen (although it is most always the user's misuse of variable

```
INVOCATION:
INTEGER      Var_Int_Average(Number_of_Integers, Array_of_Integers)
INTEGER      Number_of_Integers,
INTEGER      Array_of_Integers.


INTERNAL:
INTEGER      Running_Sum,
INTEGER      Counter.

FUNCTIONS:
LOOP: BEGIN
        Counter (1 .. Number_of_Integers)
        Running_Sum = Running_Sum + Array_of_Integers[Counter]
        END

ARITHMETIC:
        Running_Sum = Running_Sum / Number_of_Integers

RETURN:
        Running_Sum.
```

Figure 17.3   Function pseudo code.

```
int     Var_Int_Avarage (int Quantity, int *Integers)
{
long    running_sum;        /* Running sum of the integers.    */
int     counter;           /* Loop counter                    */

        running_sum = 0;

        for (counter = 0; counter < Quantity, counter++) {
                running_sum += (long) Integers[counter];
                }

        return (int) (running_sum / (long) Quantity);
        }
```

Figure 17.4   C language implementation.

types and type casting). The revision that made it to the top and is considered to be the reusable object must be identified with a version label. It is now in production.

Now that the module is ready, it needs to be made available to all users. In the personal computer realm, the way to share the module is by adding it to a library file. A library file is a collection of object modules. An object module is the result of running a compiler on a source module. Figure 17.5 illustrates the path from source code to membership in a library file. The source module is compiled producing an object file. A library maintenance program is then run that adds the object file to the library. The library is then placed in a common directory to which every programmer has access. We have now created a reusable object.

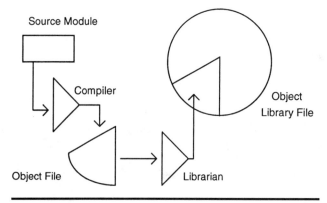

Figure 17.5   Storing a reusable program code object.

Maintaining the Reusable Object

Once the reusable object has been created, it must be maintained. As new releases of the compiler used to make the reusable objects are made, the reusable objects must be recompiled and combined into a new revision of the library file. Sometimes bugs are discovered. Sometimes the unpredictable is uncovered.

For whatever reason, whether it is a single object or the entire library that must be reconstructed, the new revisions of the source modules should be identified with a version label. If all the existing modules are recompiled due to a new compiler release, then no new source revisions exist. However, a new release of the library exists. The revisions of the source modules used to construct the new library should be identified as belonging to that library. A single source revision may represent many library releases. The same holds true if only one or two modules are altered and a new release of the library is made. The new revisions will be identified as belonging to the new version of the library along with the revisions that were not altered.

Figure 17.6 illustrates a manner under which library files and archive files for a library can be stored hierarchically. All library files, regardless of function or content are stored in a one or more library file directories. One directory may store all libraries or only those libraries specific to a project. A subdirectory of the "VCS" directory could be the "Libs" subdirectory, Under the "Libs" directory are "Library_Name" subdirectories, each representing a library of objects.

Reusing the Reusable Object

Whenever programmers wish to use a reusable object, they must do two things. First, reference the function or procedure from the library

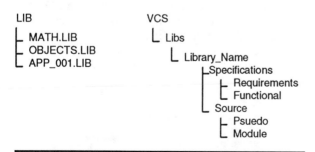

Figure 17.6 Library files and archive directories.

that they wish to use in a source module. That is, make the call and use the procedure. The second thing that must be done is to reference the name of the library from which the object is extracted on the link command line (or in a build script).

If the referenced object is one that is used to replace another object and the object to be replaced is a member of a standard or application library, then the link command line must reference the new object's library before the library in which the old object resides. Merely adding the new library name to the list of libraries will not suffice. The linker will search the libraries in the order they are listed for objects and as soon as an object is found, the linker will use it. When two objects have the same name, the object from the library listed later will never be used.

Summary

The reuse of code modules in the form of object files and libraries can provide application developers with pretested functions that do not need to be redeveloped for the application. The ability to reference code segments that do not need to be developed can result in reduced time to market and increased profitability. Once the reusable object has been created, it becomes available for any program that requires its functionality.

Questions

1. As stated above, some modules are not suitable for reuse, such as a parser. What other types of modules would not be suited for reusable status? Why?

2. In some development environments, each time that a function is needed for an application, that application receives its own unique coding of the function. The same function may be written over and over again. In fact, some programmer's make a career out of rewriting the same modules over and over again. What would such a programmer think of a reusable object? Would the programmer perceive reusable code as a career threat? What could be done to convince the programmer of the value of reusable code?

18

Complying with ISO 9001

The International Standards Organization, (ISO), has for many years set standards for systems operations. These standards run the gamut from the length of a meter to how to define and use virtual devices in a computer graphical application interface. One of the proposed ISO standards is ISO 9001, dealing with quality systems. Basically, what ISO 9001 does is provide an developmental model for ensuring quality assurance during the software life cycle. The model contains rules for maintaining records during the design, development, and production stages of a software application as well as rules for installation and servicing of complex systems. Some of these rules specifically call for the use of configuration management techniques.

This book is not an appropriate forum for discussing all of the aspects of the ISO 9001 standard. However, those aspects which are governed by configuration management are well worth considering. According to ISO 9001, configuration management is a method for identifying, controlling, and tracking the official versions of a software item. We all know by now that this is rather a minimal definition. ISO 9001 also specifies that early versions of a software item that are still in use should also be maintained and controlled. If we have practiced configuration management as defined in this book, we will meet this requirement with ease.

Let us examine some of the requirements for a configuration management system as defined by ISO 9001 and see how they are met by using the PVCS series of products.

Requirements

Software Items

According to ISO 9001, a configuration management system should be able to uniquely identify the official versions of each software item. A software item is a single module. As each official version of the item is released, the revision of the module that is in the new official version is identified by a unique version label. Perhaps *Alpha* for the alpha release, *Beta* for the beta release, and so on. Using PVCS version labels provides the configuration management system with the ability to uniquely identify all official versions of all software items.

Product versions

The configuration management system should provide a mechanism by which the revisions of software items that when combined produce a specific version of the complete product can be identified. This requirement is also fulfilled by using PVCS version labels. As each version of the complete product is released, the respective revision of each module used to construct the complete product is identified by a unique version label. Even if the release goes to only one customer, that release can be identified by a version label and reconstructed at any time.

Build status

The configuration management system should be able to identify the build status of software products from the development stage through delivery and installation. Under PVCS, this requirement can be met in several ways. In general, and most simply, the use of promotion groups provides the ability to determine the status of modules. By determining the promotion group of a revision, one can determine where in the life cycle the revision of the module resides. A more complicated method would involve the use of version labels used to describe the status of a revision of a module.

Asking if the revision is in "Test," "Debug," "Production," and so on is asking the build status of the module. If promotion groups are used, the answer is found by examining the name of the group to which the revision belongs. If version labels are used as well, the answer can be much more precise.

Simultaneous update

The simultaneous update problem was discussed in Chap. 1. It is one of the fundamental problems solved by one of the most basic configuration management paradigms. The requirement as specified in ISO 9001 is that the configuration management system should control the updating of a software item by more than one author. The simultaneous update problem is solved using locks and branches. If a user owns a lock on a revision, than no other author may check in a new revision until the lock is removed, then the new author may obtain a lock.

Multiple updates

The configuration management system should, according to ISO 9001, provide a method of coordinating multiple product updates from one or more locations or sites. This requirement can be met using the "VDIFF" and "REGEN" PVCS utilities. The "VDIFF" command is used with the "-d" option so that it creates a delta script. The delta script identifies the changes from one specified revision to another specified revision. The "REGEN" command is used with the delta script to modify a module of the first specified revision to produce the second specified revision.

The "VDIFF" and "REGEN" commands will not provide a method of coordinating the release to the various sites, but will coordinate the actual update to those sites.

Change requests

ISO 9001 specifies that change requests be maintained and tracked. Even if the change request originates as a suggestion, it should be tracked from it origin. All change requests should be tracked up to and through release into the product.

If change requests are processed through a database, then that database should be modified so that it is capable of maintaining the various revisions of the change request. If possible, change requests should be also maintained under PVCS. If the database does not change daily, then the database file could be stored under PVCS. If no database system is available to track the change requests, then the change requests should be maintained under PVCS as individual files.

Specifications

ISO 9001 requires that all functional and technical specifications for a module be maintained in a manner such that the functional and technical specifications for a version of a module can be identified. This is consistent with the recommendations put forth in this book. The archive file for the specification can have version labels just like the archive file of the specified module. As each version of the module is identified, that version label can be assigned to the appropriate revision of the specification.

Tools

Any and all development tools that affect the function and or technical specification of a module should be identified for each version of a module. This is also consistent with the recommendations put forth in this book. One revision of one module may compile differently under different versions of the same compiler. An easy way to accomplish this requirement under PVCS is to first identify all tools used in a build script. The build script is stored under PVCS and, as new releases of the product are made, new version labels are assigned to the appropriate revision of the build script. When a tool changes, say a compiler is updated, the new version of the tool is stored in a unique directory. The build script must be modified to identify the new directory name. The revision of the build script identifies the exact tools used in the creation of that particular version of the product. The revision of the build script is assigned a version label exactly as the source modules are. Now, not only can we identify the revisions of the modules used in a release, but the revisions of the tools used to make that release.

Interfaces

Most software modules interface to other software modules or to hardware. ISO 9001 specifies that these interfaces be identified for each version of a software item. Typically, such identification is embodied in the source code itself. Under a loose definition of terms, it could be said that the ability to retrieve the revision of the code associated with a version provides the exact interface used by that version of the module in that the code itself specifies the interface.

Documents

ISO 9001 specifies that all documents and other computer stored files related to a version of a software item be identified. Unfortunately, there is no automated way of accomplishing this task. One suggestion would be to reference documents that have to do with the specifications of a module in the archive file description entered when the archive file is first created. Any new documents can be referenced in the change comments entered when the alterations specified by the new documents are implemented in a revision. Another suggestion would be to reference all documents from specification to user manuals in the product build script.

Change Control

The configuration management system should provide a mechanism by which any changes to any software module can be identified, documented, reviewed and authorized. These four requirements are met by various features of the PVCS series of products. Any alteration of a module can be identified by a revision. Each revision has a change description. Each module must pass its quality-control tests and be promoted either by promotion group, version label, or both. This ensures that each module change is reviewed. And finally, only users with the correct authorization (permission) can promote the module. Thus, the promoted revision can be said to have been authorized.

Validity

The ISO 9001 standard states that before a change is made official, its validity should be confirmed and any effect on any other module should be identified and examined thoroughly. This amounts to testing the module and generating and studying a where used document. Affected modules should be tested to verify that their operation remains unchanged.

Notification

The ISO 9001 standard specifies that some method exist by which any changes made to an item would cause any person concerned to be notified of said changes. Additionally, some traceability between the changes and the modified parts of the software module should be provided.

Setting up a notification system is not very difficult providing that some tools exist to facilitate its implementation. For example, if the network has some form of electronic mail, then the build script can be modified such that if a change in a module, code, or specification is detected, an electronic mail message is sent to some specified person. There can be some real benefits if a little extra work is put into setting up the system. For example, if a module changes, the documentation group could be automatically notified so that they can verify documentation against the new changes. Or, if a specification changes, the programmer can be automatically notified so that he or she can then examine and alter the module as necessary to conform to the new specification.

The "VDIFF" command provides the mechanism by which the exact changes made to a module in any given change can be determined. The user simply identifies the initial revision and the revision that resulted from the change and a complete and exact report will identify exactly all the changes made to the module.

Summary

Very few extra tasks need be accomplished above and beyond the everyday use of PVCS to provide ISO 9001 compliance. It is fortunate that PVCS provides such vast functionality in the configuration management arena as correct use of the product line can provide complete software configuration management in a networked development environment.

Index

About the Author

Joseph H. Rawlings III has more than 25 years of experience writing computer programs. He is currently an independent consultant and an expert on SCM. He developed his expertise in this area as Training Manager for Polytron Corporation, the original developers of PVCS Versions Manager and PVCS Configuration Builder products. As a consultant, he provides management, security, and other team design consulting services and holds more than 300 software copyrights.